YEARS OF

ELECTRICS

Tim Wheeler of Ash on stage with his Jet

YEARS OF

ELECTRICS

HALF A CENTURY OF WHITE FALCONS, GENTS, JETS & OTHER GREAT GUITARS

TONY BACON

50 Years of Gretsch Electrics

Tony Bacon

A BACKBEAT BOOK

First edition 2005

Published by Backbeat Books

600 Harrison Street

San Francisco, CA 94107, USA

www.backbeatbooks.com

An imprint of The Music Player Network, United Entertainment Media Inc.

Published for Backbeat Books by Outline Press Ltd,

2A Union Court, 20-22 Union Road, London SW4 6JP, England

www.backbeatuk.com

ISBN 0-87930-822-2

EDITOR Siobhan Pascoe
DESIGN Paul Cooper Design

Origination and Print by Colorprint (Hong Kong)

05 06 07 08 09 5 4 3 2 1

contents

The Gretsch Story

Chet Atkins, the most important guitarist in Gretsch history

It was 50 years ago that the Gretsch company launched its two most famous electric guitars, the spectacular White Falcon and the cowboy-flavoured Chet Atkins Hollow Body, or 6120 as it's usually known. In the decades since, all manner of players have discovered and revisited these two classics – as well as many of the other Gretsch models – and in recent years new reissues and near-equivalents have been launched by a revived Gretsch operation, now run in tandem with Fender.

For years the company catalogues and ads have proclaimed that it's all down to "That Great Gretsch Sound". But just what is that sound? And is it great? Well, it's raw. It has a certain clarity, but it's a growl, it's grainy, it's gritty. Pick up a Gretsch and you might experience that famous tendency to feedback, or there's a chance you'll be confused by some baffling controls. No two old Gretsches sound or feel alike: 'inconsistent' is probably the most polite description you'll come up with. Crazy gadgetry. Cool beauty. Weird tone. Stylish glamour. That's Gretsch for you. And this book celebrates the 50-plus years that the electrics have been around us, with stories of all the great guitars, the players who've learned to love them and continue to discover their idiosyncratic charms, and the people who design, make and sell them – back then as well as right now.

GERMANY CALLING

First, though, we need to travel in time, right back to the middle decades of the 19th century. In the United States, foreign-born immigrants were pouring into the country, and Germany was the main source of this increasingly big injection of new blood, well ahead of Italy, Ireland, Russia and Scandinavia.

One such middle-class German émigré was Friedrich Gretsch, the son of a grocer from Mannheim in central Germany. Friedrich was only 17 when he sailed from Germany to America in May 1873. He settled in New York City and took a job with a drum and banjo manufacturer, Albert Houdlett & Son – despite the fact that his Uncle William, with whom he lived in Brooklyn, had a successful wine business there. Clearly, Friedrich was already determined to go his own way. He further staked his independence by anglicising his forename, and in 1883 left Houdlett to set up his own business: the Fred Gretsch Manufacturing Company. He produced drums, banjos, tambourines and toy instruments at the firm's small premises on Middleton Street in Brooklyn, selling to local musical-instrument wholesalers such as Bruno or Wurlitzer.

Friedrich's son Fred, the eldest of seven children, had been born in 1880, and at age 15 had an unexpectedly swift introduction to his father's music business. Friedrich had returned to Germany in April 1895 for the first time since his emigration, but on the way to a meeting with a brother in Heidelberg he died suddenly in Hamburg, at the age of just 39. Another son, Louis, later recalled the shock of his father's unexpected demise. "The first word the family received after he sailed for Europe," said Louis, "was a cable reporting his death and burial."

Friedrich's widow Rosa decided that 15-year-old Fred should leave his studies at Wright's Business College for an immediate and practical immersion into the real world of commerce. Teenager Fred found himself heading up a still modest operation with about a dozen employees, now based in a converted wooden stable on South 4th Street. There is a story that whenever Fred Gretsch took a customer to lunch in a nearby Brooklyn bar, the waiter would take one look at the youngster and say, "No matter what you order, you're going to drink milk." Fred seems to have ignored these ageist remarks, and instead made a virtue of his youth by channelling that teenage enthusiasm into the growth and expansion of the Fred Gretsch Manufacturing Company. Apparently he would regularly venture out on to the roof of the building to help with the tanning of hides for drum skins. By 1900 Fred – today usually referred to as Fred Sr – had added mandolins to the company's drum and banjo-making activities. Gretsch's original cable address, 'Drumjolin', alludes to this early trio of manufacturing interests. Fred had begun to import musical instruments from Europe, too, for example introducing the excellent K Zildjian cymbals from Turkey to the US market. Also at this time he moved the company to better premises in a small three-storey building once again on Middleton Street in Brooklyn.

Two of Fred Sr's brothers joined him in the business after the turn of the century: Louis Gretsch went on the road selling instruments for a year before giving up his one-third interest to become a real-estate agent, while Walter Gretsch lasted longer, leaving in 1924 with a salesman colleague to establish Gretsch & Brenner, a small company importing musical instruments that lasted into the mid 1950s.

Meanwhile, Fred Sr continued to expand the Gretsch company successfully in the early years of the 1900s. In 1916 construction was completed on a large ten-storey building at 60 Broadway, Brooklyn, alongside the approach to the Williamsburg Bridge that crosses the East River to connect Brooklyn to Manhattan in New York City. This large, imposing building would house the factory and offices of the Fred Gretsch Mfg Co for many years to come. By the early 1920s Gretsch was advertising an enormous and flourishing line of instruments, primarily using Rex and 20th Century as brandnames. There were banjos (the most popular stringed instrument of the time), mandolins, guitars, violins, band (wind) instruments, drums, bells, accordions, harmonicas, gramophones, and a variety of accessories such as strings, cases and stands. Company secretary Emerson

> **In 1883 Fred Gretsch left the Houdlett drum and banjo firm to set up his own business, the Fred Gretsch Manufacturing Company, and was soon producing drums, banjos, tambourines and toy instruments on Middleton Street in Brooklyn.**

Strong told *Musical Merchandise* in 1925: "We have more than 150 workers in the plant and are increasing production as each year passes."

At the end of the 1920s and into the early 1930s the guitar began to replace the banjo in general popularity as a more versatile and appealing instrument. It was in 1933 that Gretsch started to use its own name as a brand for guitars. The company offered a line of archtop acoustics, the Gretsch American Orchestra series, as well as a handful of flat-top acoustics, including the Gretsch Broadkaster model. These guitars were not especially unusual or notable, and it wasn't until the Synchromatic line more or less replaced the earlier guitars in 1939 that pros began to take Gretsch acoustics seriously. The Synchromatics were bigger and louder, had distinctive styling, including cat's-eye or triangular soundholes, and into the 1940s brought Gretsch a sound reputation alongside the better-quality instruments of the market leaders, Gibson and Epiphone.

Gretsch offered the acoustics among a still burgeoning wholesale list of other brandnames, including guitars bought in from the 'big two' Chicago makers, Kay and Harmony. Gretsch themselves manufactured instruments for other outlets, including mail-

INTO THE 50s WITH GRETSCH ELECTRICS

Spotlight on AL CAIOLA

Top CBS Guitarist Caiola, plays a heavy radio and TV schedule appearing with Archie Bleyer, Ray Bloch, Alfredo Antonini; records steadily as well. Al says the "Miracle Neck" of his *Gretsch Electromatic Guitar* (with twin Gretsch-DeArmond pickups) cuts down the tension of his heavy schedule, keeps his hands fresh for show-time: "Fastest, easiest-playing, richest-toned guitar I've ever owned." Write today for more about this sensational Gretsch innovation—plus the *Gretsch Guitar Guide*, yours FREE. Address: The Fred. Gretsch Mfg. Co., 60 Broadway, Brooklyn 11, N.Y. Dept. DB-452.

CAN YOU NAME THIS CHORD?

Al Caiola's hand curves for a stretch that could seem a challenge after a day's workout on an ordinary guitar. The slim, slim *Gretsch Miracle Neck* literally gives his fingers extra length, makes playing easier-faster. Try this chord on your own guitar now—then visit your Gretsch dealer and try it on the new Miracle Neck guitar. You'll be amazed at the difference!

▾ **1955 Streamliner**

◀ **1954 Electro II**

◀ **1955 Corvette**

As Gretsch entered the 1950s its sole electric guitar was the Electromatic Spanish model, as featured in the 1950 catalogue (far right). It was replaced four years later by the similarly non-cutaway Corvette (left), maintaining the basic, spartan feel and including a DeArmond single-coil pickup. The Electro II (far left) was one of Gretsch's first cutaway electrics and was endorsed by session player Al Caiola (top left). The Electro evolved into the well known Country Club model in 1954, represented here by a Cadillac Green example (opposite, top) and one in rare light/dark grey finish (opposite, main guitar). They mark Gretsch's early and influential use of striking colours for some models. The ideas-man behind many of the Gretsch electrics was Jimmie Webster, pictured (top right) playing an Electro II.

▲ **1955 Country Club**

◄ **1956 Country Club**

Spotlight on JIMMIE WEBSTER

JIMMIE WEBSTER DELIGHTED RECENT TV VIEWERS of the Arthur Godfrey and Sheriff Bob Dixon shows with his amazing "touch system" of guitar playing which reverses completely all usual fingering methods. Jimmie, famous as guitar teacher, innovator and M.C., says, "My new Gretsch Synchromatic Guitar with *Miracle Neck* is the fastest, easiest-playing guitar I've ever handled." Send for the FREE *Gretsch Guitar Guide* that gives you valuable

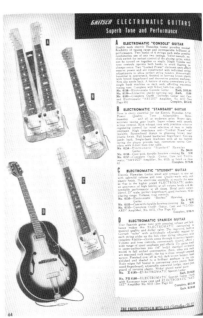

order catalogue companies such as Montgomery Ward and Sears, Roebuck. Altogether, the Gretsch operation marketed a multitude of musical merchandise including drums, guitars, banjos, mandolins ... in fact virtually anything that might be played by the budding musician of the time. Around 1930 the company had spread its distribution still wider across the US by opening a Midwest branch in Chicago, headed by Phil Nash. In combination with the factory and office in New York City this provided an efficient and profitable business network right across the country: the New York office covered the area from the East Coast to Ohio, the Chicago office from Ohio to the West Coast.

The first 'Spanish' electric guitar bearing the Gretsch brand was offered by the company around 1939. (By 'Spanish' we mean a regular guitar, as opposed to a lap-steel Hawaiian type.) It was called the Electromatic Spanish and was made by Kay in Chicago; Gretsch simply added a headstock veneer with their logo. It was virtually identical to the instrument that the Cleveland-based Oahu company sold as their Valencia model at the same time. The Gretsch had a non-cutaway, archtop, laminated body with f-holes and checkerboard binding, and there were coloured position dots on the fingerboard. It had a simple single-coil pickup near the neck and, unusually, the volume and tone knobs were mounted on opposite sides of the upper body, each side of the neck. This would certainly not be the last time that a Gretsch guitar would have controls situated in an unconventional position.

> "The guitar you play is a definite factor in the quality of the music you produce. A Gretsch guitar truly glorifies the talents of the artist who commands it." *Fred Gretsch Jr.*

The Electromatic Spanish came complete with an amplifier for $110, but made little impact on the market, if indeed it was sold in any quantity at all. Electric guitars were still in their infancy and not yet well understood by makers or players. Electric Hawaiian guitars had turned up earlier in the 1930s. Regular Spanish archtop acoustic guitars with built-in electric pickups and associated controls had been made by Rickenbacker, National, Gibson and Epiphone at various times during the decade, but with little impression on players. That didn't stop one Dick Sanford and Clarke Van Ness from composing a song in 1940 called 'When I Play On My Gretsch Guitar', recorded by singing cowboy Red River Dave and including the unforgettable refrain: "When the shadows grow / And the lights are low / Then I play on my Gretsch guitar. / As I touch the strings / Like a voice it sings / It's the voice of my love afar."

When the United States entered World War II in 1942, Gretsch's Spanish electric guitar was quietly dropped. Changes were happening elsewhere in the company. Fred Sr was still nominally president, but had effectively retired from active management in the early 1930s to devote himself entirely to banking, the business he really loved. He officially retired from Gretsch in 1942, and died ten years later. He was replaced as company president in '42 by his third son, William Walter Gretsch – generally known as Bill – who had taken over the Chicago office in the mid 1930s. Bill headed the business until his premature death at the age of 41 in 1948. His brother Fred Gretsch Jr, already the company's treasurer, then took over as president. Fred Jr would steer Gretsch through its glory years in the 1950s and 1960s.

During World War II, Gretsch continued to make some musical instruments but concentrated on government war contracts, among other things manufacturing circular wooden hoops for use in gas-masks. Of course, many Gretsch personnel were called up for active service, but the company was able to return to full instrument production during the years from 1946, gradually re-organising itself into a firm ready for the new challenges ahead in the 1950s.

Charles 'Duke' Kramer was an important recruit. He'd started working for the Midwest office in Chicago in 1935, first as a purchasing agent and later as a salesman. After a wartime stint in the army Kramer returned to his job with Gretsch in Chicago, taking over the running of the branch when Bill Gretsch died in 1948.

"When we all came back from the services," Kramer told me, "we had a meeting in New York in 1946 to determine whether we wanted to continue as a jobber-distributor type operation, or whether we wanted to go major line and sell product under the Gretsch logo. Up to that time we had been making drums and guitars mostly for other people. So we decided we wanted to go major line. We couldn't do both immediately, so we started out in drums, and in 1947 and 1948 we introduced the Gretsch drum line. It was very shortly after that when we started to make our first electric model guitars."

Gretsch needed new people to promote these new lines, hiring Phil Grant to look after drums and Jimmie Webster for the guitar side. Grant was a professional drummer who played with the Pittsburgh Symphony and the Edwin Franko Goldman band. Gretsch pioneered and developed the plywood shell and introduced smaller-size bass drums and decent hardware, going on to produce some superb drums in the 1950s and 1960s that are still revered by players today. Webster was a professional piano-tuner, pianist and guitarist – and, as we shall discover, would have far-reaching and profound influences on the development of Gretsch's electric guitar lines.

Grant told me about his first years at Gretsch and the changes happening to the business in the late 1940s. "The Gretsch company did carry on as a jobber – that is, a wholesaler who sells miscellaneous things to retail stores – and so that part of the business never really changed for us: Monopole band instruments, LaTosca accordions, Eagle strings, that kind of thing. It was just that on the drums and guitars we stopped selling to catalogue-houses and people like that who were only interested in low-price merchandise. We decided to go and shoot for the big stuff, and so the low-price items sort of faded into the background."

YOUR GRETSCH GUITAR GUIDE

Gretsch issued an 18-page brochure around 1950, *Your Gretsch Guitar Guide*, that talked up the company's new emphasis on guitars for professionals, and among other things publicised Gretsch's new and generous three-year guitar guarantee, which covered any defects caused by faulty workmanship or defective materials. "The guitar you play is a definite factor in the quality of the music you produce," Fred Gretsch Jr wrote from his office in the Gretsch Building on Broadway, Brooklyn. And he couldn't resist adding a final flourish: "A Gretsch guitar truly glorifies the talents of the artist who commands it." Over the top, for sure, but it showed that the company was serious and fired up about its new guitar models.

The first post-war Gretsch electric guitar revived the Electromatic Spanish name, debuting in 1949 alongside a number of Synchromatic-series acoustic guitars. The electric had a non-cutaway archtop body with f-holes, at first finished in sunburst and later also in

◄ 1955 Silver Jet   ◄ 1960 Jet Fire Bird   ◄ 1955 Duo Jet

▲ Jeff Beck's 1956 Duo Jet

JET BLACK & THE ROCKABILLY REBELS

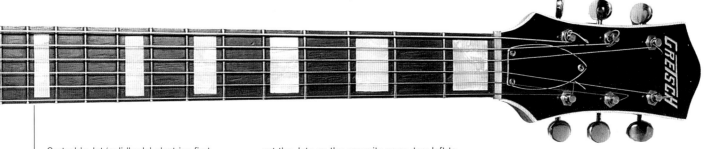

Gretsch's Jet 'solidbody' electrics first appeared in 1953 in the shape of the black Duo Jet, like Jeff Beck's '56 pictured here (main guitar). Jeff is a big fan of the finest player to put his hands on the Jet in the 50s, Cliff Gallup, seen above (main picture) with his boss Gene Vincent and the rest of the Blue Caps. Gallup played a remarkable series of cameo solos on sides such as 'Be Bop A Lula' and 'Race With The Devil', leaving Vincent in late '56 for obscurity – but Gretsch nuts and rockabilly rebels will never forget him. Check out the Jets on the opposite page, too: left to right there's a luscious Silver Jet, the first of Gretsch's sparkly jobs, a red Jet Fire Bird model that debuted in '55, and an early black Duo Jet. Gretsch's catalogue page from '55 (right) also includes the orange Round Up. Another fine 50s player of the Jet was Hank Garland, pictured opposite in another of Gretsch's 'Spotlight' ads. Better known for his later involvement in Gibson's Byrdland, Garland was a talented player in the territory where country meets jazz.

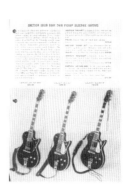

natural. It had a single-coil pickup, described in the catalogue as a "built-in Gretsch mike". This would become famous as Gretsch's DeArmond pickup, made for them by Rowe Industries of Toledo, Ohio, a company run by Harry DeArmond. The unit featured six polepieces in a distinctive black-topped chrome case, with a row of screws to allow each polepiece to be individually adjusted for height. It would be used by Gretsch until the late 1950s, and although a 1951 catalogue listed it as the "Gretsch-DeArmond Fidelatone", a few years later the pickup officially received its more familiar Gretsch name, the DynaSonic.

At $110 the 1949 Electromatic Spanish was competing with similarly basic electric instruments of the period such as Gibson's $137 ES-150 model. These were non-cutaway guitars – a body design that already seemed old fashioned. Gibson had led the way in cutaway-body electrics with the ES-350 Premier model of 1947, and the wider acceptance of electric instruments was beginning to make a cutaway body a necessity. Why? Well, there was little point in playing high up the fingerboard on an acoustic – the results were just unlikely to be heard. But on an instrument equipped with a pickup and suitably amplified, a cutaway offered easier access to the now more audible and musically useful upper reaches of the board.

So it was that Gretsch issued its Electromatic and Electro II cutaway-body electrics in 1951. In effect, Gretsch was stating publicly that it really did take seriously the new electric guitar business. "Electric guitar at its peak!" proclaimed an ad for the new twin-pickup $355 sunburst Electro II ($20 more for the natural version) complete with gold-plated hardware. Again, it was aimed to compete with the market leader, Gibson, whose comparable ES-350 was selling for $385 ($400 natural) in the early 1950s.

JIMMIE WEBSTER PRESENTS ...

Gretsch's new hollowbody electric cutaway models were first presented to professional guitarists and music dealers at a three-day promotional show held at New York's Park Sheraton Hotel in January 1951. *The Music Trades* magazine reported that Gretsch's event enjoyed excellent attendance by "many top-flight guitarists" and described it as "an exciting forerunner of the important position the new Gretsch [models] will hold". Demonstrating the latest electrics as well as a number of acoustic models at the hotel launch was Jimmie Webster, described in the report as Gretsch's "special representative".

Webster was born in 1908 in Van Wert, Ohio, and later moved to Long Island, New York. He played piano and guitar and worked in the 1930s as a musician in nearby New York City. He also made money as a qualified piano-tuner, and at one stage ran a music store, as had his piano-playing father, Harry. Webster's mother Kathryn also played and taught piano. Sometimes when money was tight she had accompanied silent movies at the local cinema.

Webster had been casually involved with Gretsch before World War II, but it was in about 1946 that he began to work regularly for the company. His daughter, Jennifer Cohen, who was born in 1948, told me: "He used to do so many things, and when I was growing up he started to work more for Gretsch. He began to travel a lot for them, promoting the guitars. I don't think he was ever exclusively a Gretsch employee, he just regularly billed them for his services, more like a freelance. He wanted to call his own shots and run his own life, and he always said he never wanted to be tied to them – that was his personality. So he worked several days of the week for Gretsch, and on alternate days he tuned pianos. Monday, Wednesday and Friday he would go into Gretsch in Brooklyn; Tuesdays and Thursdays he would tune pianos around the small town we lived in on Long Island. He was very much in demand as a piano tuner, very popular." He seems to have been popular with his colleagues at Gretsch, too. Phil Grant's comment – "Jimmie was a wonderful guy, and very smart" – is typical.

As we shall see, Webster became Gretsch's main ideas man, bombarding management and production teams with all manner of guitar models and add-on gadgets in an effort to distinguish Gretsch's instruments from the growing competition. Webster would also travel around the US, and occasionally abroad, to promote the latest items at trade fairs, as well as at public shows. We'd call these a clinic today; Gretsch called them a 'Guitarama'. Webster was a great find for Gretsch: a musician, an inventor and a salesman, all wrapped up in one likeable, outgoing personality. He probably did more than anyone else to spread the word about Gretsch guitars, and became a travelling ambassador for Gretsch, for electric guitars, and for guitar playing in general.

Webster's own playing style was unusual, and the company made a plus of this too, often using space in catalogues and brochures to explain about the 'Touch System'. This was also a specific peg on which Gretsch could artfully hang general publicity for their guitars: a 1952 ad, for example, mentions appearances by Webster on a couple of TV shows where he would show off "his amazing Touch System of guitar playing".

> **Jimmie Webster probably did more than anyone else to spread the word about Gretsch, and soon became a travelling ambassador for the electric guitar.**

What was the Touch System? Modern readers will probably recall the 'tapping' technique that Eddie Van Halen did much to popularise in the 1980s. Well, Jimmie Webster employed a similar idea back in the 1940s. He would produce chordal rhythms with his left hand using a sort of rapid hammering-on motion and, without a pick, would simultaneously play the melody by tapping the strings against the upper fingerboard with his right-hand fingers, adding a bassline with his thumb. "It's like patting your head and rubbing your stomach at the same time," Webster joked.

His use of the Touch System probably had quite a lot to do with the fact that he was at heart a piano player. Several people told me that Webster was a better pianist than guitarist. Presumably it seemed natural when he played guitar to use both hands in a somewhat similar manner to the way he would on piano. Many of those who heard him play said that at first they couldn't believe that all the sounds were coming from one person playing one guitar, that it seemed like at least two guitarists.

"Credit for the discovery of the Touch System belongs to Harry DeArmond," Webster admitted in a 1950 Gretsch brochure, "whose name you probably recognise since he manufactures the popular and powerful DeArmond pickups." It's been suggested that DeArmond developed the system to demonstrate his pickups – which, as we've already learned, Gretsch used on their electric guitars in the 1950s. Webster insisted: "Professional players like the Touch System because it gives them a whole new field of solo possibilities. People who play for their own amusement and for their friends find the guitar now more complete within itself than ever before." This was optimistic. The style did

1955 Chet Atkins ►
Hollow Body 6120

America's big favorite
CHET ATKINS raves about
his new Gretsch Guitars

From Grand Ole Opry
in Nashville to Boston,
Mass. and clear across
the country, Chet Atkins'
very special brand of
guitar playing has won
an enthusiastic audience.
(Hear his RCA album, "Stringin'
Along With Chet Atkins.")
We're proud that Chet praises the
playing ease and tone of his two
Gretsch guitars — uses both the hollow
body and the solid models, "depending
on the type of work I'm doing."

For information on these new
"Chet Atkins Country Style"
Electromatic Guitars, write to
FRED. GRETSCH, Dept. DB 1185,
60 Broadway, Brooklyn 11, N. Y.

THE FRED. GRETSCH MFG. CO.

CHET ATKINS ELECTRIC GUITARS
by GRETSCH

CHET ATKINS SOLID BODY GUITAR

CHET ATKINS HOLLOW BODY GUITAR

CHET'S G-BRAND ON A HOLLOW BODY

▲ 1956 Chet Atkins Solid Body 6121

▲ 1954 Chet Atkins prototype

1955 Chet Atkins ▶
Hollow Body 6120

Chet Atkins was becoming well known in the 1950s (see 1956 cutting, far right) for his easy-on-the-ear style served up with a relaxed delivery that disguised a prodigious technique. Gretsch's Jimmie Webster persuaded Chet to put his name to the company's first 'signature' guitar, the Chet Atkins Hollow Body 6120, launched in 1955 in the wake of Gibson's successful Les Paul model. A prototype (main guitar) was based on the earlier Gretsch Streamliner and differs from production models with its flat tailpiece and belt-buckle decoration. Also different from regular 6120s is the early version (left) sent to Chet, with its altered control layout. This first-year model (right) shows all the proper features, including Bigsby vibrato. A 'Solid Body' 6121 version (top) is seen in an ad with Chet and in a 1955 catalogue alongside the 6120 (far right).

not catch on at the time, although Webster continued to use it happily and effectively for decades. It wasn't until that high-volume application of a similar concept by Van Halen in the 1980s – by which time Webster had been dead for a number of years – that tapping techniques had their moment of fame.

During the first few years of the 1950s, Gretsch was content to offer a selection of four electric archtop models, but the company was no doubt keeping an eye on the moves being made by other manufacturers towards the development of a solidbody electric instrument. During 1950, Fender in California was the first to bring a commercial product of this type to market. Gretsch certainly noticed this, because Fender called its new solidbody electric the Broadcaster, a name that Gretsch still used (spelled Broadkaster) for a number of drum products.

> Country music was gaining in popularity – Hank Williams even had pop hits in 1953 – and so Gretsch aimed its new Round Up model squarely at the rising number of country guitarists, adorning the instrument with unrelenting Western decoration.

Fender salesman Dale Hyatt told me about the reaction from Gretsch. "There was a camaraderie between the manufacturers in the early days and no one was trying to beat the other to a patent or anything like that. So Gretsch just pointed it out and we agreed to change it." At Gretsch's request Fender thus dropped the name of their innovative Broadcaster, and from 1951 it became the Fender Telecaster. At first most guitar makers considered Fender's electric solidbody a small-fry manufacturer's oddity that probably would not last. But attitudes changed relatively quickly.

Gretsch were certainly surprised when they saw their chief rival produce a solidbody electric guitar in 1952, the Gibson Les Paul model. Ted McCarty, Gibson's president from 1950 to 1966, said that Fred Gretsch Jr was amazed that such a traditional company as Gibson should be involved in this modern nonsense. "When we introduced the Les Paul at the trade show," McCarty told me in 1992, "Fred Gretsch, who was a personal friend of mine, said, 'How could you do this? Why and how could you do that for Gibson?' We were good friends, and I said, 'Fred, somebody's got to stop this guy Fender, he's just about trying to take over.' Fred said, 'But Ted, anybody with a band-saw and a router can make a solidbody guitar, and I just can't believe that Gibson would do it.'"

Fred Gretsch Jr overcame his initial outrage when he noticed that Fender and Gibson were actually beginning to sell quite a few of these new-style electrics, and the businessman in him took over. In 1953 Gretsch launched its first solidbody, the $230 Duo Jet. In fact, while the guitar looked like a solid and certainly recalled the general outline and visuals of the $225 Gibson Les Paul, underneath things were somewhat different. At the time, Gibson used a sturdy sandwich of mahogany and maple for the Les Paul's body, while Fender used solid ash for its Telecaster. Gretsch, however, assembled the just-over-13-inches-wide body of the Duo Jet from several pieces of mahogany, incorporating a number of routed channels and pockets for cables and components, and adding a pressed arched top as a 'lid'. The most accurate description of Gretsch's new 'solid' guitar is probably 'semi-solid'. But in terms of its look, function, catalogue description and intended place in the market, the Duo Jet was in effect Gretsch's first solidbody electric guitar, as Duke Kramer confirmed. "A lot of people called it a semi-solid, because we routed out an awful lot of space in the wood for the electronics," said Kramer. "But basically we considered it a solidbody guitar."

Unusually, during its early years the new Duo Jet's body had a front covered in black plastic material, as used on some Gretsch drums. The guitar's control layout marked the start of Gretsch's fondness for positioning a master volume knob down on the cutaway bout rather than with the other controls (and the Electro II gained one of these around the same time). Early Gretsches with DeArmond pickups almost always have a layout of four knobs and one switch. At the bottom of the body are three controls: nearest you a volume for the neck pickup, then a bridge-pickup volume, and, furthest away, an overall tone knob. On the cutaway bout is a master volume, and on the top bout a three-way both-or-either pickup switch.

The Jet came with Gretsch's unique two-piece strap buttons – an early take on the idea of locking strap buttons. One part of the button was screwed into the body so that the hole in the strap could be placed over the protruding threaded spigot, and then a knurled knob was screwed down to hold the strap securely in place. The model also featured the Melita Synchro-Sonic bridge, which had been a feature of some Gretsch electrics since the previous year.

JOHNNY MELITA'S METAL SCULPTURE

The Melita Synchro-Sonic was the first guitar bridge to offer independent intonation adjustment for each string, meaning a guitar potentially more in-tune with itself than a regular bridge allowed. It beat Gibson's more famous Tune-O-Matic version by at least a year. The design was brought to the company by Sebastiano 'Johnny' Melita, who subsequently manufactured the units for Gretsch in his own workshops. It's an apparently complex mass of chrome-plated metal that looks as if it might be more at home on a saxophone, but Gretsch immediately recognised the Melita's potential to provide the more accurate intonation that was required on electric guitars. Loosening one of the easily accessible row of six top-mounted screws allowed the attached saddle to be moved back or forward in order to set optimum intonation for that string. In a June 1952 ad, Gretsch promoted the Melita as "for the first time" offering "perfect tuning and clearer high notes" thanks to its "separate adjustable saddle for each string [that] permits split-hair tuning".

Early in 1954 two further 'solidbody' electric models in the style of the Duo Jet were added to the line: the country-flavoured Round Up; and the sparkle-finished Silver Jet. Country & Western music was spreading in popularity – Hank Williams even had hits on the pop charts in 1953 – and Gretsch aimed the Round Up squarely at the rising number of country players by adorning the guitar with unrelenting Western decoration.

It had a steer's-head logo on the headstock and pickguard. Various Western motifs – mostly steer's heads and cacti – were engraved into the block-shape fingerboard markers. A belt buckle with a homely wagon-train scene was attached to the tailpiece. There was even a big 'G' for Gretsch actually branded into the front of the Western orange-finish body, which had metal-studded leather stuck around its sides embossed with yet more cacti and steer's heads. And to hang all this from the shoulders of the adoring new owner, the guitar came with a leather strap encrusted with rhinestones and decked out with the obligatory steers and cacti. Subtle it was not. Gretsch took to optimistically describing the Round Up as having "masculine beauty". Almost equally unsubtle was the Silver Jet, also

CAN WHITE GUITARS PLAY THE BLUES?

▲ 1956 White Penguin

▼ 1955 White Falcon

A—Gretsch "Convertible" Electric No. PX6199 in two-tone Copper Mist and Lotus Ivory (See Page 4)

B—Gretsch "Corsair" Arched Body Guitar No. X6016 in Bordeaux Burgundy (See Page 11)

C—Gretsch "Fleetwood" Custom Built Guitar No. X6038 in shaded brown and amber (See Page 8)

D—Gretsch "Country Club" Electric Guitar No. PX6196 in Cadillac Green (See Page 4)

E—Gretsch "Rancher" Jumbo Flat Top Guitar No. X6150 in Western finish (See Page 13)

F—Gretsch "Corvette" Electric Guitar No. X6184 in Jaguar Tan Finish (See Page 4)

G—Gretsch "White Falcon" Electric Guitar No. PX6136 in white and gold (See Page 2)

H—Gretsch "Streamliner" Electric Guitar PX6190 two-tone Copper Mist and Bamboo Yellow (Page 5)

GUITARS FOR MODERNS BY Gretsch

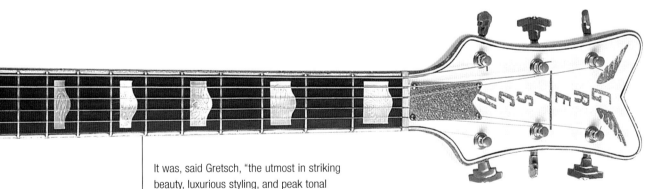

It was, said Gretsch, "the utmost in striking beauty, luxurious styling, and peak tonal performance". Players had to agree that the $600 White Falcon was a stunner, as this launch-year 1955 example (main guitar) testifies. This one is relatively plain given what was to follow. The Falcon's mutant offspring was the peculiar 'solidbody' White Penguin (top left) which drew so little interest at the time that it's now considered the rarest and most collectable Gretsch of all. The 1955 catalogue cover (above) was a glorious affair that celebrated the company's increasingly colourful models, including the new Falcon.

launched in 1954, which came with a silver sparkle finish on the body front, obviously a by-product of Gretsch's drum department. Drum boss Phil Grant told me it was Jimmie Webster's idea to use drum coverings on some of the guitars. "We would buy our plain, pearl and sparkle drum covering in plastic sheets from a local company called Monsanto, and Jimmie went into the factory one day and could see we were making drums with it. He said, 'Well, why can't we make guitars with it?' So we did! We would glue the plastic covering to the body, just like you do on a drum shell. Maybe the acceptance wasn't 100 percent out there in the field, but they were good looking guitars."

In a busy year for the inventive guitar department, Gretsch also revised its line of archtop electrics. The non-cutaway Electro II was dropped, while the three other models were renamed. The non-cutaway 17-inch-wide-body Electromatic Spanish became the Corvette; the 16-inch Electromatic became the Streamliner; and the cutaway 17-inch Electro II became the Country Club. Most guitar makers have trouble thinking up model names, but it's unusual to reveal the thought process in public. Nonetheless, Gretsch prematurely announced the renamed Electro II as the 'Country Song' guitar in an October 1953 ad. In fact, when the properly named Country Club appeared in 1954 it heralded the start of a 27-year run that would make it the longest-lived model name in Gretsch's history – and one that would be revived in 1996 and 2001.

IN LIVING COLOUR

Another significant addition to the way Gretsch marketed its guitars came in 1954 with the option of coloured finishes for some models, beyond the regular sunburst or natural-wood varieties. We've already noted the company's use of drum coverings on the sparkly Silver Jet and the early black Duo Jet, but equally flamboyant paint finishes were on the way.

Automobile marketing was having a growing influence on guitar manufacturers in the early 1950s, and the theme was especially evident in Gretsch's colourful campaign of 1954. The company announced a Cadillac Green option for the Country Club and a Jaguar Tan (dark gold) finish for the Streamliner. The paints came from DuPont, which also supplied most of the car companies (and later Fender too). Gretsch again drew on the experience it had of finishing and lacquering drums in different colours, applying knowledge and skills that already existed within the company to help the guitars stand out in the marketplace.

There were only isolated precedents for coloured guitars, including Gibson's gold ES-295 and Les Paul of 1952, and Fender's infrequent custom colours, soon to be spurred to official status by Gretsch's influence. But for a few years Gretsch made the use of colour into a marketing bonus almost entirely its own, adapting car-industry finishes for guitars, and no doubt prompting the wild visuals of Harmony's Colorama guitars introduced in '55. Through the middle 1950s, Gretsch added a number of pleasant two-tone options – yellows, coppers, ivories – by contrasting a darker body back and sides against a lighter-coloured front, mimicking the style of flat-top acoustics.

This was yet another idea that came from long-standing techniques used in Gretsch's drum department. With an eye on the TV boom of the 1950s, Gretsch vice president Emerson Strong told a reporter: "These colour combinations are likely to become even more effective as colour television receivers are installed and the public grows increasingly accustomed to the bright hues they will see on their screens every day."

By March 1954, Gretsch's guitar pricelist boasted a respectable line-up of six electric guitars (alongside eight acoustics from $52.50 to $475). There were three archtop electrics: the Corvette at $137.50 sunburst, $147.50 natural; Streamliner $225 sunburst, $235 Jaguar Tan (dark gold), $245 natural; and Country Club $375 sunburst, $385 Cadillac Green, $395 natural. There were also three 'solidbody' electrics: the black Duo Jet at $230 (with four-string baritone ukulele and tenor guitar options listed at the same price); the new Silver Jet at $230, and the orange Round Up at $300.

The success of Gibson's Les Paul guitar – well over 2,000 were sold in 1953 alone – alerted other manufacturers, including Gretsch, to the value of a 'signature' model endorsed by a famous player. Today the practice is very familiar – overdone, perhaps – but back in the 1950s it was a new, exciting and, for the companies, potentially profitable area of musical instrument marketing. A signature guitar named after a musician was a step beyond the kind of advertising that Gretsch was already running, which simply highlighted the use of the company's guitars by particular players.

Gretsch's New York-based ad agency, Mitchell Morrison, had devised a series of 'Gretsch Spotlight' ads that appeared in musicians' publications and trade magazines in the early 1950s, featuring mainly jazz and studio guitarists such as Al Caiola (with an Electro II), Mary Osborne (with a Country Club) and Hank Garland (with a Duo Jet). Phil Grant, who liaised between Gretsch and Mitchell Morrison, said: "Every musician liked a little publicity. They figured it would help them with their career: your name and picture in the papers. But to be honest Al Caiola had a limited following, he would only be known to studio musicians, and Mary Osborne was pretty much the same, though of course she had the glamour angle. Really those ads didn't have much impact, they were just a name and a picture."

LESTER FOR GIBSON, CHESTER FOR GRETSCH

What Gretsch needed was their own Les Paul – in other words a well-known player whose name they could put on an instrument and use to attract fresh, untapped interest in their guitars. Around 1954, Jimmie Webster came up with the answer: Chet Atkins. It was a solution that in time, directly and indirectly, would turn Gretsch's fortunes around.

While still in his early 20s back in the 1940s, Chester Burton Atkins had landed a recording contract with RCA, and was soon playing electric guitar backing the Carter Sisters and others on Nashville's *Grand Ole Opry* stage. His career had developed quickly on both sides of the recording studio glass.

Chet would go on to help create the so-called Nashville Sound when put in charge of RCA's new studio there in 1957, while making his own instrumental gems – from 'Main Street Breakdown' to 'Yakety Axe' – that had guitarists everywhere slowing record-players down a notch to try to work out how he managed his impressive, apparently effortless and influential multi-line picking style.

But in the mid 1950s he was still busy making his mark as a talented Nashville-based country guitarist. "I was already doing well at the time Gretsch made their approach," Atkins told me when we met in Nashville in 1995. "I was on the Opry, I was playing on network radio shows, and I think I was already on national television then – Jimmy Dean had a show on CBS and he'd have me on every once in a while. I was pretty popular nationally when I went with Gretsch." He remembered Jimmie Webster contacting him in

DOING THAT ROCK'N'ROLL THING

Bo Diddley bought a Jet Fire Bird ... and, hey Bo Diddley, here he is playing it (left) with a jacket to match. Those innovative colourful finishes were making waves for Gretsch in the 1950s, attracting rock'n'roll players like Bo with an eye for a natty look. He also had Gretsch make him a bizarre guitar with a rectangular-shape body after his own woodworking skills proved lacking, and the Gretsch growl accompanied him on stage as well as on record. A few years later, another Gretsch fan landed a Duo Jet. In 1961 George Harrison, lead guitarist for a cocky new outfit called The Beatles, saw an ad in a Liverpool paper posted by a sailor who'd bought a Gretsch in America. George swiped the Duo Jet (below) and used it all on his group's early recordings. It would not be his last Gretsch.

▲ 1958 Duo Jet

A youthful Duane Eddy (left) proudly plays his brand new Chet Atkins 6120 towards the end of 1957, and the actual instrument is pictured (right). He would use the Gretsch on many of his instrumental hits from the 1950s onwards, and the 6120 played a significant part in the creation of Duane's signature 'twangy' tone, a deep and dark sound very different from that used by the instrument's originator, Chet Atkins. The 6120 also found favour with another leading player of the period, Eddie Cochran (below). Underrated as a guitarist, Cochran is best known for his pop hits, but was a fine, talented instrumentalist.

◄ Duane Eddy's 1957 Chet Atkins 6120

▼ George Harrison's 1957 Duo Jet

Nashville at a time when he was using a D'Angelico Excel acoustic cutaway archtop to which he'd added a Gibson pickup. "I had seen people playing Gretsch guitars, a couple of my friends played them," said Atkins.

"Then Jimmie Webster would come to town to demonstrate Gretsch guitars, and he wanted me to play them. They had some design, but I didn't like it. But he kept after me. I remember once he took me over to a music store to try some things – he really wanted me to play one of their guitars. So finally he said, 'Well, why don't you design one that you would like?' He invited me out to the factory in New York."

The suggestion interested Atkins, and he made some preliminary enquiries. "Les Paul had his endorsement with Gibson and so I called him – he and my brother Jimmy had worked together in a trio. I said to Les, 'How much royalties should I get?' He hummed and hawed around, finally gave me a number, don't know if it was right or not. Then someone else said to me, 'Why don't you get a lawyer to go with you?' But I didn't do that, I was afraid a lawyer would queer the deal by asking too much or something. When you're young like that, money doesn't matter."

An insider remembered the deliberations that went on at Gretsch concerning the deal. "When Jimmie Webster first mentioned that we ought to get someone like Chet Atkins to endorse the guitar, Mr Gretsch said, 'Why should I pay a hillbilly guitar player to use his name on our guitars?'"

But Webster obviously managed to persuade Fred Gretsch Jr of the advantages. Soon after the suggestion from Webster, Atkins flew up from Nashville to New York City for a meeting at Gretsch. "I went over to Brooklyn to the factory," recalled Atkins, "and visited with Mr Gretsch, Emerson Strong, Jimmie Webster and Phil Grant. They were very nice, and we came up with the design for the orange Gretsch Chet Atkins. I think if Jimmie Webster were alive today he would tell you the most important thing he ever did was to sign me, because they started selling the hell out of guitars."

The prototype for the Chet Atkins Hollow Body 6120 model was made probably in 1954, before the model name had even been finalised. The label inside identified it as a Streamliner Special. "That's the first one I received," Atkins explained. "They sent it to me and said, 'How about this?' But I wanted a Bigsby vibrato on it, and I especially didn't like the f-holes, and later on we changed those. They also put all this junk on it, the cattle and the cactus, which didn't appeal to me at all."

CHET'S WESTERN PARAPHERNALIA

Gretsch had reckoned that with Chet's country connections there was an opportunity to re-use the Western decorations they'd devised for the Round Up guitar. As Duke Kramer described it: "Instead of giving a pair of cowboy boots with every guitar, we put this Western stuff on it." Despite his strong reservations about the Western paraphernalia, Atkins gave in. "I was so anxious to get my name on a guitar, so I said oh … that's fine. I was thrilled to have my name on a guitar, like Les Paul had his name on the Gibson. At the time I was full of ambition and I wanted to be known all over the world as a great guitarist, and that was one brick in the edifice that would help that happen."

The Western decorations would be gradually removed from the original Chet Atkins models over the following years. Gretsch also gave ground by adding a Bigsby vibrato to the production model, in line with Chet's request. As well as the Hollow Body 6120 model with 16-inch-wide body, Gretsch issued the Chet Atkins Solid Body 6121, essentially a Round Up with a Bigsby vibrato replacing the belt-buckle tailpiece (and, despite the name, the Solid Body still had Gretsch's customary semi-solid construction). The two new guitars were announced, with a hazy idea of the model names, in the December 1954 issue of *The Music Trades* under the heading 'Gretsch To Have New Guitars, Chet Atkins Country Style'. The news item read: "Chet Atkins, top favorite of the Grand Ole Opry and one of the nation's best guitarists, plays and endorses the new Gretsch 'Chet Atkins Country' model guitar. Chet Atkins Country Style Electromatic guitars are available in the conventional hollow body or the solid body. Both have Gretsch DeArmond built-in pickups, slim, fast playing Miracle Neck, and built-in vibrola. Both models will be available for delivery after January 1, 1955, and are priced at $360 list (case extra)." That $360 would amount to about $2,540 translated into today's buying power.

> "Chet Atkins was the greatest thing that ever happened to us. The Gretsch Chet Atkins models put us on the map." *Phil Grant, Gretsch vice president*

Atkins had little to do with the Solid Body model, and it has since been described by one Gretsch insider as a "mistake". The guitar was quietly dropped after a few years. The Hollow Body model, however, became for a while Atkins's exclusive instrument for his increasingly popular work, and would go on to become one of the most revered Gretsch models. The Hollow Body has become more generally known by its Gretsch model number, 6120, and so in a modest bow to tradition that is exactly what we shall continue to call it in this book.

Have you noticed how there's often a divide between what the endorsed guitar company sees as right for the market and what the endorsing player requires personally from an instrument? Les Paul, for example, would invariably modify his namesake models that Gibson supplied to him. Chet Atkins, reflecting in 1995 on his original Gretsch guitars of the mid 1950s, told me that he too wasn't entirely happy with what he was given. "I played that orange Gretsch 6120 guitar, but I hated the sound of the pickups at first," he said, referring to the single-coil DeArmond DynaSonics fitted to all early 6120s. "The magnets pulled so strong on the strings that there was no sustain there, especially on the bass." Chet would have to wait until 1958 for a change in that department.

Meanwhile, Gretsch was happy to see the effect of the new endorsement deal. The 1955 catalogue trumpeted: "Every Chet Atkins appearance, whether in person or on TV, … and every new album he cuts for RCA Victor, wins new admirers to swell the vast army of Chet Atkins fans." Phil Grant, Gretsch vice-president at the time, said later: "I think the following that Chet had in country music surpassed even Les Paul's general following. You can't undervalue Chet's importance – he was the greatest thing that ever happened to us. The Gretsch Chet Atkins models put us on the map."

Not content with the coup of attracting Chet Atkins to the company, Jimmie Webster was experimenting during 1954 with ideas for a guitar that would become Gretsch's top-of-the-line model. "I have a feeling the White Falcon was his dream guitar," Webster's daughter Jennifer told me. "I remember when he was developing it there was talk that this was going to be something real special."

Special it certainly was. The White Falcon was first marketed by Gretsch in 1955, and it was an overwhelmingly impressive instrument. The 17-inch-wide single-cutaway

1958 Chet Atkins 6120 ▶

Gretsches were changing as the 1950s wore on, as this 6120 (left) shows. Now the guitar has little of the earlier Western decoration, or "junk" as Chet himself later described it. Instead it has 'half moon' or 'Neo-Classic' fingerboard markers, Gretsch's new Filter'Tron humbuckers, designed by Ray Butts, and the associated two-knob controls and two-switch tone circuitry.

◀ **1957 Clipper**

▲ **1957 Streamliner**

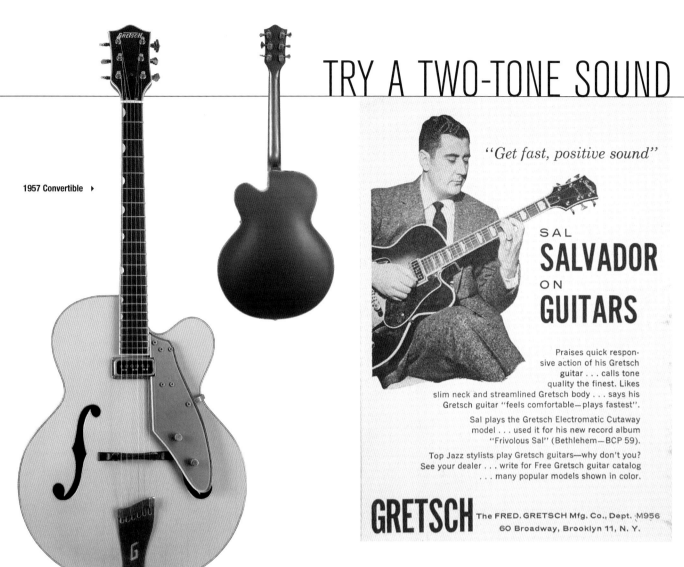

1957 Convertible ▶

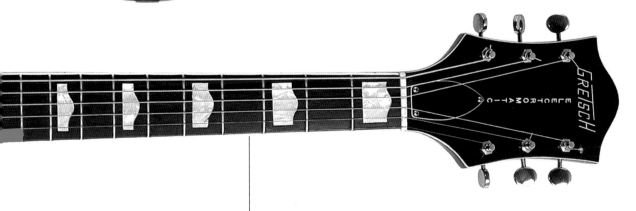

Gentle two-tone finishes graced many a
Gretsch in the 1950s, like the three guitars
shown with backs across these pages. This
Streamliner is in a pleasant yellow/brown
combo and displays the 'hump top'
fingerboard markers of the period, while the
cheaper cream/grey Clipper (top left) has dot
markers. The Convertible (above) had a pickup
and controls fixed to the pickguard rather than
the body, and was later renamed for its best
known player, Sal Salvador (top right).

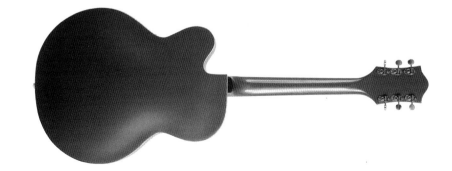

archtop hollow body was finished in a gleaming white paint finish, as was the new 'winged' headstock. Both had gold sparkle decorations, again borrowed from the Gretsch drum department. All the guitar's metalwork was gold-plated, including the fancy Grover 'stair-step' Imperial tuners and the stylish new tailpiece, since nicknamed the Cadillac because of its bold V-shaped decoration similar to the car company's logo. The new 'hump-top'-shape fingerboard markers had suitably ornithoid engravings, and the gold plastic pickguard featured a flying falcon about to land on the nearby Gretsch logo. It was, quite simply, a stunner.

"Cost was never considered in the planning of this guitar," boasted the Gretsch publicity, and it's hard to disagree. "We were planning an instrument for the artist-player whose caliber justifies and demands the utmost in striking beauty, luxurious styling, and peak tonal performance, and who is willing to pay the price." To be precise, the new Falcon's retail price was $600 (equivalent to about $4,200 in today's money). The next highest in the Gretsch line at the time was a $400 Country Club. Gibson's most expensive archtop electric in 1955 was the $690 Super 400CESN – and while a fine instrument, it was by comparison a sedate, natural-finish product of the relatively conventional Kalamazoo-based company. Meanwhile, over in New York, Gretsch proclaimed the idiosyncratic White Falcon as "the finest guitar we know how to make – and what a beauty!"

> "Fred was forced to go into production on the White Falcon – which he didn't want to do, because it's a miserable guitar to make."
> *Duke Kramer, Gretsch*

For Jimmie Webster, a white guitar was not such a new idea. His daughter Jennifer kept a picture of her father playing in his Army Air Corps band during World War II, and in it he was clearly using a Harmony guitar with a white finish. Even more intriguing among Jennifer Cohen's collection of memorabilia was a 1943 newspaper cutting sent home by Jimmie during the war. Cohen said: "He's mentioned in the article, and there's a little arrow pointing to 'me'. Then if you flip it over, you can see that this forces newspaper is called *The White Falcon*. I really think that's where the name for the guitar came from."

Another influence on the style of the White Falcon may have come from the banjos that Gretsch marketed – they had for example acquired the Bacon & Day banjo company in the late 1930s. Some of the more ostentatious models had gold trim, fancy fingerboard markers, and rhinestone inlays. It's fair to deduce that some features of the White Falcon – including its distinctive jewelled knobs and feathery fingerboard inlays – may well have been inspired by Gretsch's banjos. There's no reason to suppose that borrowings would be limited to those from the drum department, and Jimmie Webster was probably fond of wandering around the entire factory in his search for new ideas.

"We were always looking for something new to bring out at the NAMM conventions," said Duke Kramer of the White Falcon. At these important regular gatherings of the National Association of Music Merchants the major manufacturers would show their new models, usually in advance of them appearing on the market, and dealers would visit from all over the country to decide which of the new wares they would eventually want to stock in their stores.

An early White Falcon prototype was displayed at one of Gretsch's local promotional events in March 1954, but the guitar's first big showing was at the major NAMM show in

Chicago four months later. Gretsch enticed store-owners by billing the still experimental Falcon as one of the 'Guitars Of The Future' along with the green Country Club and the dark-gold Streamliner.

"We followed the automobile industry," explained Kramer. "General Motors had what they called the Autorama show where they would display a dreamlike, futuristic car model. We felt we could do that on a guitar. So we made the White Falcon for the show. It created quite a stir. We had it on a turntable with spotlights on it and it looked very special. Because of the response at that show, Fred was forced to go into production on the Falcon – which he didn't want to do, because it's a miserable guitar to have to make."

Phil Grant also remembered the Falcon's reception among the music store owners, and how this flagship model became a help to Gretsch's general marketing efforts. "Our sales force always had a struggle getting our guitars accepted, because Gibson were number one," he said. "So if Gibson had one dealer in a city, we had to look to find a dealer that wasn't quite as hip and quite as knowledgeable to put our guitars in. And of course the best dealers in town would obviously have Gibson. It became easier when Jimmie Webster got the thing going and we had the White Falcon and guitars like that. The dealers were getting calls for the Falcon, and when that happens they're a little more agreeable to putting in stock."

Gretsch began to supply dealers with the first Falcons in 1955, and the influence of this spectacular new model even spread to other guitar manufacturers. Don Randall, head of Fender's sales department at the time, told me that Gretsch's coloured guitars influenced Fender to officially offer in 1956 their 'player's choice' colour options, known from the following year as Custom Colors. "I was out in the field and sales oriented," explained Randall, "so I saw that Gretsch had their green Country Club and the White Falcon. We offered our colours to diversify and get another product on the market." He also said that, despite earlier Gretsch and Gibson models featuring gold-plated hardware, it was the White Falcon that finally alerted Fender to the visual bonus of sparkling golden metal. "We couldn't be outdone," was Randall's analysis – and from around 1957 Fender began to offer some of their models officially with the option of gold-plated hardware.

THE PENGUIN GOES STRAIGHT

In the same way that Gretsch had issued a companion 'solidbody' to the Chet Atkins 6120 model, they also produced a partner to the White Falcon in the company's semi-solid style. This was called the White Penguin. It came complete with all the Falcon features and was first released in 1956. "The name came about because a penguin has a white front," insisted Duke Kramer, although it's hard to imagine how Gretsch expected anyone to buy a guitar with such an unappealing and comical name. It even had a little penguin waddling across the pickguard.

Sure enough, very few people bought the White Penguin. It didn't appear in any of the company's catalogues, and only made a fleeting appearance on one pricelist (in 1959, at a steep $490). From the small number that surface today, it's likely that very few Penguins were made, and the model has since become regarded as one of the most collectable of all Gretsch guitars. So the occasional examples that do turn up command very high prices: a 1957 White Penguin was sold in 1992 for a staggering $70,000, and then five years later a '58 example went for $75,000. With that guitar, said Stanley Jay of New York

Gretsch chose to mark its 75th birthday in 1958 by launching the budget-price Anniversary with one or two pickups (both pictured, right). Perhaps the only hint of luxury that one might reasonably expect on an anniversary was the attractive two-tone green finish. The model would be further downgraded in the early 1960s when the unbound ebony fingerboard was replaced with cheaper rosewood and the Filter'Tron humbuckers turned into single-coil HiLo'Trons.

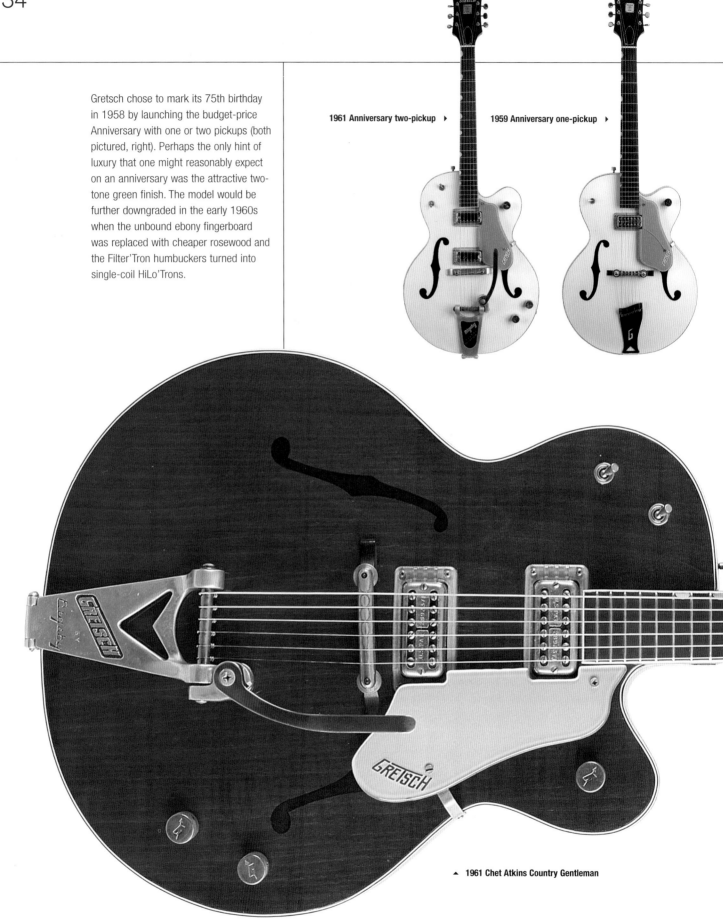

1961 Anniversary two-pickup ▶

1959 Anniversary one-pickup ▶

▲ 1961 Chet Atkins Country Gentleman

THE GENTLEMAN HAS ARRIVED

1960 Chet Atkins ▶
Tennessean

MONO RD-27214 (LPM-2232)   CHET ATKINS' WORKSHOP   RCA RECORDS

CHET ATKINS' WORKSHOP

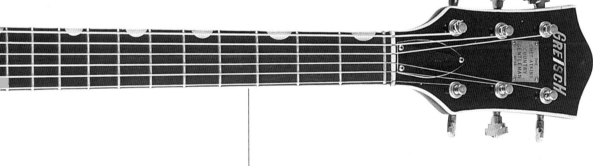

Two new Chet Atkins models debuted in 1957 and 1958, the two-pickup Country Gentleman (main guitar) and the single-pickup Tennessean (top). The Gent had 'fake' f-holes because Chet figured that a 'sealed' body would reduce nasty feedback. Somewhere a teenage Neil Young planned revenge, but Chet (far right) used a Gent for many recordings. The Tennessean for now sported a single humbucker – like Chet's on the '60 sleeve (above). Gretsch meanwhile were busy promoting the unique style of their guitars, as in this page from the 1959 catalogue (right).

dealer Mandolin Brothers, "we broke the world's record for the sale of a fretted instrument not previously owned by a deceased superstar".

When it came time for Gretsch to compile the 1955 catalogue they decided to pull out all the stops and create a document that would show off their new models and bright finishes to best effect. They produced a striking brochure with a cover that, unusually for guitar companies at the time, was in full colour. Over the outside front and back covers they displayed eight vivid models, including Convertible and Streamliner in two-tone finishes, a green Country Club, a dark-gold Corvette and, of course, a White Falcon. Gretsch also took the opportunity to parade in colour the two orange Chet Atkins models on the inside front page, plus the black Duo Jet, orange Round Up and the recently added red Jet Fire Bird on the inside back. "One look at these new Gretsch guitars will tell you why musicians all over the country are raving about them," wrote Jimmie Webster inside, gazing out at the reader from behind his Country Club. "Whether you play hillbilly, jazz, progressive or just plain strum an' sing, there's a Gretsch guitar for you," he continued, modestly hinting that Gretsch now had lines that catered for virtually all the guitar-playing tastes of the era.

> The White Penguin didn't appear in any of the company's catalogues and only made a fleeting appearance on one pricelist, in 1959, at a steep $490. From the small number that surface today, it's likely that very few Penguins were made.

As the number of electric guitar models increased and the profile of the company was raised by glossy new brochures and popular endorsers, Gretsch decided to employ a quality-control person to ensure that what was coming out of the factory was equal to all this fresh attention. The new man to join the guitar team at the Brooklyn factory in 1956 was 24-year-old Dan Duffy, who'd been studying guitar with New York jazzman Sal Salvador. Salvador played a Gretsch Convertible, a 17-inch-body guitar introduced in 1955 and so-called because, like many early electrics, its pickup and associated controls were 'floating' on the pickguard, thus avoiding interference with the resonance of the archtop body and, as Gretsch put it, "preventing the combination of electric and acoustic properties". Salvador became so associated with the Convertible that towards the end of the 1950s Gretsch renamed it the Sal Salvador model.

"Constantly in touch with Gretsch, Salvador knew that they wanted a young, keen player like Duffy to work as a quality controller. Duffy told me about the set-up at the factory when he started. "I was in the small assembly department where they put the pickups and tailpieces on, strung the guitars up, tuned and adjusted them. It was up on the ninth floor of the ten-storey Gretsch building. Guitars were made on two of the floors at that time; the rest was let to other people. Next door to us was the machine shop where they made bridges, tailpieces and so on, and then next to that was the plating department.

"Down on the seventh floor was the wood shop and the finishing room, where they sprayed the guitars," Duffy continued, "and beyond that area at the time was the shipping department, which dealt with Fred Gretsch's wholesale business: accordions, banjos, band instruments, that type of thing. The other part of the seventh floor was taken up with the drum department. As the years went by, the drums were moved out, the finishing department became immense, and guitars were made throughout the whole area. But that's how it was in the 1950s and into the first part of the 1960s."

Duffy emphasised the key role played by the foremen throughout the Gretsch factory. So often, manufacturing histories concentrate on the management figures and top people, whereas the products that define a firm's success wouldn't exist without the skills of the workers on the shop floor.

"Probably Fred Gretsch's success was due to surrounding himself with good players and good foremen," Duffy suggested. "When I got there some of those guys had already been there 25 years. They were super-mechanics, experienced tool-and-die makers. They were devoted to him and to that company." He runs through a roll-call of some of the foremen who made Gretsch guitars happen: Vincent DiDomenico and Jerry Perito (in the wood shop); Jimmy Capozzi (in plating); Sid Laiken (machine shop); Johnny DiRosa (finishing); Felix Provet (assembly); and Carmine Coppola (repairs). "We all got along so great," Duffy reminisced. "If we had problems with rejected guitars, finishes, whatever, everyone would help out everyone else. It was like one big family."

SCRATCHES, DENTS, AND OK CARDS

When Duffy was interviewed at Gretsch for his quality-control job in 1956, Jimmie Webster explained to him a new system of cards they would use to keep a running check on a guitar's progress through the factory. Each 'OK Card' had checks for Finish, Workmanship, Construction, Nut, Bridge, Action, Intonation, Electrical Equip[ment], and Playing Test, plus a space for a quality controller's signature at the bottom. "Throughout the years," recalled Duffy, "we had a quality-control meeting once a week where each foreman would discuss any problems. There were always finishing problems: scratches, nicks, dents, dust in the finish that had to be buffed out. Then in the wood shop the hand-sanding had to be perfect: the better the wood is sanded, the better the finish lays on. There were periods where we had neck-pitch problems, wood shrinkage problems, and binding problems, especially on the White Falcon guitars. But we tackled that whole thing together. There was a lot of talent in that company, and that's what made it work."

Some of Duffy's "problems" from back then are what make each vintage Gretsch guitar a potential surprise today. Anyone who has played more than a few old Gretsches will be aware of this – and some might put it less charitably. It's the frustration of never being sure what to expect, of knowing that you are just as likely to find yourself struggling with a poor instrument as rejoicing at how well this gem of a guitar plays. That's old Gretsches for you.

But as Duffy concluded: "You go into a guitar store and you buy a name. But if only you realised what went into that guitar, all the lives and the years that guys took to make those guitars the way they were. And it wasn't Fred Gretsch Jr, as much as we loved him. It was the guys who got there every morning at six o'clock. They did it. You remember that."

Back in October 1956, prices for Gretsch's 11-model electric guitar line were detailed in a catalogue bound into the latest issue of *Country & Western Jamboree*. There were six archtops: the Clipper at $175 in sunburst or $185 in two-tone Desert Beige/Shadow

> Anyone who has played more than a few old Gretsch guitars will know the frustration of never being sure what to expect. That's old Gretsches for you.

SIX STEREOPHONIC STRINGS

◄ 1958 White Falcon Stereo

▲ 1959 White Falcon (mono)

GRETSCH GUITARS

THE FRED. GRETSCH MFG. CO. GRETSCH GUITAR CATALOG No. 30

▼ **1958 Country Club Stereo**

The White Falcon continued as Gretsch's lavish flagship, but 1958 saw a new option for the Falcon and Country Club: stereo! The idea, a Gretsch first, was to split the pickups so that the sound of one set of three strings went to one amp and the other three to another amp. Despite a later updated system, some beautiful catalogue covers (1961, above) and a stereo LP by Jimmie Webster (opposite) it was too complex for most players and quietly faded away. But the Falcon, of course, lived on.

Metallic Gray; Streamliner $250 sunburst, $260 two-tone Bamboo Yellow/Copper Mist, $260 natural; Convertible $320; Chet Atkins Hollow Body 6120 $400; Country Club $400 sunburst, $420 Cadillac Green, $420 natural; and White Falcon $650. Five semi-solids completed the picture: the Duo Jet at $290; Jet Fire Bird $300; Silver Jet $310; Round Up $350; and Chet Atkins Solid Body $400.

ROCK'N'ROLL IS HERE TO STAY

One new musical category that Jimmie Webster failed to mention in his round-up of guitar styles in that '55 Gretsch catalogue was rock'n'roll. Hit records through 1956 and '57 for Chuck Berry, Bill Haley & His Comets, Buddy Holly, Jerry Lee Lewis, Carl Perkins, Elvis Presley and others would spread the popularity of this new musical phenomenon, one that would eventually sweep the old guard from the map and put American teenagers at the helm as the course was set for modern pop music. None of the guitar companies chased rock'n'roll guitarists to play this or that guitar back then at the birth of the music. Instead, Gretsch, Gibson, Guild and the rest mostly concentrated on established jazz, country and studio pickers. But Gretsch gained enormous benefit from some unsolicited associations with successful artists in the early years of rock'n'roll, and two of the most important used Chet Atkins 6120 models to power their sound.

Eddie Cochran was a talented, accomplished guitarist. He started out as a session player, but his moody good looks landed the 18-year-old a cameo spot in the 1956 Jayne Mansfield movie *The Girl Can't Help It* where he performed 'Twenty-Flight Rock'. Cochran subsequently made some blasting rock'n'roll singles including the classic 'Summertime Blues', a US number 8 in 1958. His music was a churning mix of rockabilly, country and blues played on acoustic as well as electric guitars, and at its heart was his Gretsch 6120, probably a '57 model. He continued to play sessions, and was fascinated by studio technology, employing overdubbing and other techniques before they became widespread.

Cochran might have seemed light-years away from Chet Atkins's musical stylings, and yet the youngster was certainly influenced by Chet's fingerstyle picking – and seemed to agree about the quality of DeArmond pickups, replacing the pickup nearest the neck on his 6120 with a meatier-sounding Gibson P-90. He usually played with both pickups on, achieving a very fat sound. More hits such as 'C'mon Everybody' followed, but Cochran's career was cut tragically short when he was killed at 21 in a car crash while on tour in Britain in 1960. It's instructive today to hear Cochran's lesser known material – for example the remarkable 'Eddie's Blues' from a 1959 session – because it indicates a much looser and potentially more interesting side to his playing that he might well have developed had he lived.

Duane Eddy turned out a string of hit records from the late 1950s based on his deceptively simple instrumental style that will forever be known by the word attached to so many of his albums: Twang. That twangy tone came as Eddy concentrated on playing melodies on the bass strings of his Gretsch 6120. He made full use of the pitchbending potential of the guitar's Bigsby vibrato, his amplifier's tremolo, and the studio's echo facilities, resulting in gloriously haunting hits such as 'Rebel Rouser' (a US number 6 in 1958). Eddy told me that his first decent electric guitar, at age 15, was a Gibson Les Paul gold-top. Growing up in Phoenix, Arizona, and playing in high-school bands, he would check out the local music store, Ziggie's Accordion & Guitar Studios. One day in 1957 the 19-year-old made what turned out to be a very important discovery. "I just went into Ziggie's with a friend of mine to look around," said Eddy. "My Les Paul didn't have a vibrato on it, and I wanted that bar: Chet Atkins had it, Merle Travis had it. I could play the fingerpicking thing a little, but I wanted to do the vibrato part.

"So I went in the store and looked around, and there was a White Falcon hanging on the wall, which was beautiful but it was a lot of money, nearly $700. I said, 'What have you got that's nice but not so expensive?' Ziggie pulled out two or three guitars, and the first one I opened was the $420 6120. It was the first time I saw the red Gretsch, with a Bigsby on it, and I settled on that. Took one last look at the White Falcon, but the neck wasn't as nice on it as the red Gretsch, and I didn't care for the gold trim, which looked a little chintzy. But the red Gretsch, first time I picked it up it just took to me, settled right in there, the neck was just perfect. There's nothing more exciting than finding a new guitar, but that was such an experience that I've not bought many new ones since then. I really felt no need for it." Eddy found that the 6120's DeArmond pickups suited his style well. Chet Atkins told me, laughing, "I think Duane Eddy was the only one who liked the DeArmond pickups. He got a big bass sound out of those things."

Other than some flirtations with Danelectro six-string basses in the late 1950s and a Guild 'signature' guitar for live work in the early 1960s, Duane Eddy was served well by that original Chet Atkins 6120, right through his long and successful career, until a very recent switch to Gibson. During our interview, he paused to reflect on that golden time in the late 1950s and early 1960s. "I probably sold more Gretsch guitars than anybody other than Chet Atkins," he chuckled.

GALLUP AND THE BLUE JEAN BOP

Gene Vincent and his Blue Caps hit in summer 1956 with 'Be Bop A Lula' where the beautifully concise jazz-rockabilly stylings of guitarist Cliff Gallup were first heard. Gallup's unmistakable fills and solos were there again later that year on Vincent's second single, 'Race With The Devil', and on the first LP, *Blue Jean Bop*. Gallup once said his main influences were Les Paul and Chet Atkins. He used a Duo Jet and nicknamed it his 'Pancake' for its flat top. It was probably a '55 or maybe a '56 model, complete with original DeArmond pickups and a Bigsby, and Gallup got a great sound from it.

Vincent's great guitarist has in turn influenced many, many players since, not least Jeff Beck who once said that Gallup sounded "like Chet Atkins on acid". He didn't stay long in Vincent's band, though, finding himself averse to long bouts of touring, and was gone by the end of 1956, replaced by a few short-stay guitarists and then Johnny Meeks. Gallup died in 1988 at the age of just 58, but will always be remembered by those who appreciate the art of fine – and very possibly the finest – rock'n'roll guitar playing.

One more early rock'n'roll guitar hero closely associated with Gretsch is Bo Diddley, not least for some peculiarly shaped guitars. Like many things with Mr McDaniel, it's not entirely clear how all this came about, but it seems that at one stage he may have taken the neck and pickups from a Gretsch guitar and added them to a rectangular body he made himself. Realising the shortcomings of his own handiwork, he then asked the Gretsch factory to make him a custom rectangular guitar from scratch. Bo has said this was in 1958, though it may have been nearer 1960. "It didn't record real well," he admitted

BABY YOU'RE A GRETSCH MAN

▲ 1963 Chet Atkins Tennessean

▲ 1963 Chet Atkins Country Gentleman

As the 1960s came around you could hardly avoid The Beatles. And guitarists could hardly avoid noticing that George Harrison loved his Gretsch guitars. A big Chet Atkins fan, George retired his Duo Jet when he bought a new Country Gent, just like this 1962 example (right), in time to record 'She Loves You'. By now the Gent was, like many Gretsches, a twin-cutaway guitar. After his first Gent was damaged, George got himself a replacement identical to the '63 shown here (main guitar, and with George, above). It had revised 'flip up' mute controls either side of the tailpiece. Beatle George further indulged his Gretsch habit with a Tennessean like the '63 opposite.

▲ 1962 Chet Atkins Country Gentleman

later, "so I used other guitars mostly on the records, but it was great for stage." One of the guitars he used on his early recordings was probably the Jet Fire Bird he bought from a Lyon & Healy store in Chicago. Impressed by Gretsch's work on the new stage guitar, he had them make a further oddity, with a spectacular 'winged' rocketship shape. The modern Gretsch company reissued the rectangular guitar in 1998 to coincide with Bo's 70th birthday, and the rocketship in 2005 as the Jupiter Thunderbird.

Chet Atkins was hardly oblivious to rock'n'roll: he'd played rhythm guitar on Elvis's 'Heartbreak Hotel' in 1956 and was heard more obviously on many of the hits of The Everly Brothers. But he could hardly be called a rock'n'roller. Whatever his musical role, he was still unhappy with those Gretsch single-coil pickups. Then he met Ray Butts, a music store owner and electronics wiz from Cairo, Illinois. It was an auspicious meeting: Chet's difficulties with the DeArmond pickups were about to come to an end.

RAY BUTTS BUCKS THAT HUM

Butts had gone to Nashville in 1954 to seek out the guitarists based there and attempt to interest them in his combo amplifier that offered echo from a built-in tape loop, an unusual facility at the time. Players were becoming used to echo effects in the studio, and Butts reckoned that many would jump at the opportunity to make similar sounds on stage. Chet Atkins became a customer for Butts's new EchoSonic amp – along with Elvis Presley's guitarist Scotty Moore, and Carl Perkins. Atkins got talking with Butts about other topics of common interest. Butts helped Atkins choose recording equipment for his garage studio, and then the subject turned naturally to Atkins's quest for an improved design of guitar pickup.

"Chet didn't like the DeArmond pickups that Gretsch were using at the time," Butts told me when we met at his home in 1995. "It just didn't fit his style of playing then, he said they didn't sound right. Primarily what he wanted was a proper balance between the bass and the treble and midrange, for that thumb effect he used, and he really didn't get it with those pickups. For one thing the magnets were too strong: they kept 'sucking' the strings and stopping the sustain. I saw some where he'd broken the bass-string magnets in two in a vice with a hammer. So he said to me, 'Why don't you make me a pickup?' I had done some experimenting with pickups before, so I said OK. My idea from the beginning was to build a humbucking pickup. I knew about the concept from working with transformers, and Ampex used the humbucking principle in the pickups of their recording heads. It wasn't a new idea, and it's a very simple principle."

The main intention with a humbucker pickup is to reduce the hum and electrical interference that afflicts regular single-coil pickups. The ability of such devices to 'buck' or cut hum provides their name. A humbucking pickup has two coils wired together electrically out of phase and with opposite magnetic polarity. The result was a unit less prone to picking up extraneous noise, and incidentally giving a more powerful and 'thicker' tone that some players preferred compared to the generally thinner, more trebly sound of a basic single-coil type.

Butts made a prototype and took it to Atkins, who was immediately impressed. "He showed me that pickup and I got in touch with Gretsch," said Atkins. "I told them this guy has an improved pickup that I like, that it gets the sound I want." As it turned out, the timing was dead right: a change of pickup suited Gretsch as well. Duke Kramer: "We wanted to drop DeArmond, because all of a sudden they were building pickups for anybody and everybody. It had become no great asset to have a DeArmond pickup on a Gretsch guitar, because other makers were putting them on cheap guitars as well as on expensive guitars. So we were very anxious to make this deal when it came up because we needed another pickup."

Butts went to New York to meet with Fred Gretsch Jr and Jimmie Webster at the company's offices in Brooklyn, probably some time in 1956. "They wanted to make the pickup themselves because they wanted to be sure of having supply. I wasn't experienced at manufacturing," explained Butts, "so I agreed to that. We came to an agreement on a royalty basis. I furnished all the information and everything to make the pickups, and they went and got tooling. I worked real closely with Jimmie, and I designed new control assemblies and switching to go with the new pickups."

It seems likely that the first showing of the new Gretsch-made pickup was at the summer 1957 NAMM trade show in Chicago. Gretsch was not alone in displaying a humbucking pickup: Gibson too had developed such a unit and they also probably showed it off to the instrument trade for the first time that summer in Chicago. Seth Lover, who had worked permanently for Gibson's electronics department since 1952, had been inspired to apply the humbucking principle to a pickup after seeing a Gibson amplifier that had a 'choke coil' installed to eliminate the hum produced by its power transformer.

Butts and Lover seem to have come up with their ideas for a humbucking pickup independently and at around the same time – although Lover certainly managed to file his patent much earlier than Butts. "I feel I was first with it," Butts insisted. "It's the conception that counts, and I feel I had better documentation on that. I had pictures of Chet playing a guitar with my pickups on it in 1954, for example. But Gibson complained, and Mr Gretsch discussed it with Mr McCarty at Gibson. They decided to let each go his own way without the other one challenging."

In typically grand style, Gretsch called its new humbucker pickup the Filter'Tron Electronic Guitar Head. The bombast continued in the company's explanatory leaflet: "Good electronic reproducing units such as Hi-Fidelity, Stereophonic and such, have created a demand for perfect sound and performance. ... It is with this knowledge in mind that we present the new Filter'Tron heads for guitar. The finest engineers in the country were engaged in the development of the Filter'Tron and their main object was to produce the greatest sound with as many color combinations as possible."

This patter amused Ray Butts. "'The finest engineers in the country.' That was me!" he laughed. "But they never associated me with anything, in the literature, advertising, anything else. Of course, they had their interest. But there's people to this day don't know I had anything to do with those pickups."

By 1958, Gretsch was advertising Filter'Trons as standard on all models except the thinline-body Clipper – for which the company came up with their own single-coil pickup, the HiLo'Tron. There was also a new control layout devised by Ray Butts to complement

> Ray Butts helped Chet Atkins choose recording equipment for his garage studio, and then Chet asked about the quest for a better Gretsch pickup. Butts made a prototype, and the Filter'Tron humbucker was first seen at a 1957 trade show.

I WANNA BE YOUR GRETSCH

1962 White Falcon Stereo

Anything The Beatles did, other musicians were sure to follow – or at least try. After George Harrison was seen with a Duo Jet, then a Country Gent and a Tennessean, guitarists from Los Angeles to Lyme Regis were lining up to give a Gretsch a go. Here's a few of the Brit contingent: over there (far left) we can see Chris Britton of The Troggs with a Georgealike Gent, while next door are The Yardbirds with Eric Clapton and his shortlived "too complicated" twin-cutaway 6120. Brian Jones (above) opted for the cheaper delights of a two-pickup Anniversary, managing quite nicely despite a missing knob. Gretsch meanwhile was into the second and equally unpopular phase of its stereo experiments, turning out multiple-control guitars like this Falcon Stereo (main guitar). What would Eric have made of the twin mute switches either side of the tailpiece and the four pickup and tone switches? Twin cutaways were firmly established now for most Gretsch bodies, as stylishly demonstrated with a Gent, Falcon and 6120 in the company's 1963 catalogue (right).

the Filter'Trons. A two-pickup Gretsch would now have a volume control for each pickup in the normal position at the bottom of the body, plus a master volume on the cutaway bout. On the top bout were two three-way switches: the one furthest from you was a regular both-or-either pickup selector; the other was for what Gretsch called 'tone color', selecting between neutral, bass-emphasis or treble-emphasis settings. Some of us now know this as the 'mud switch' thanks to its less than useful sounds, and most keep it permanently stuck in neutral.

INTRODUCING A COUNTRY GENTLEMAN

Two new Gretsch electric models in the Chet Atkins series were released during 1957 and 1958, the Country Gentleman and the Tennessean. "I had a hit record in the mid 1950s called 'Country Gentleman' which I wrote with Boudleaux Bryant," Atkins told me. The piece was a B-side to the 1953 single 'Bells Of Saint Mary's' (and was later re-recorded for the 1959 LP *Mr Guitar* and for an album with the Boston Pops Orchestra in '65). Bryant was a successful songwriter, well known for several Everly Brothers hits among others.

"When 'Country Gentleman' had been a hit I guess it was probably Gretsch's idea to put out another model," Atkins continued. "They were selling so many of the orange Gretsch they wanted to put out a little more expensive guitar. So the Country Gentleman had good tuning pegs, better wood selection, and the body was generally a little larger and thinner. I started to use the Country Gentleman on my records continually. I would use the 6120 once in a while – I know I've seen pictures of me with it in the studio – but I didn't use it as much as I used the Country Gentleman."

The Country Gent was Gretsch's attempt to use the Atkins endorsement to reach a wider audience than the country-flavoured 6120 allowed, and was the first Chet Atkins model to appear with the new Filter'Tron pickups. It was the first Gretsch archtop to be made with a 'thinline' body, meaning one about two inches deep, as opposed to most of the existing archtops, which measured around three inches. The thinline concept had been popularised by Gibson in the preceding years with their Byrdland and ES-350T models. The Country Gentleman was also the first Chet Atkins model to be offered with a slightly wider 17-inch body, like the White Falcon, Country Club and Convertible; the 6120 (and the new Tennessean) was closer to 16 inches wide.

Gretsch told its dealer network that "guitar star Chet Atkins will be in the Gretsch Guitar room to greet you personally" at the summer 1957 NAMM show in Chicago, where the dark brown Gent was previewed to the music trade. The retail price of $525 put the new instrument second only to the White Falcon in the company's archtop electric line.

For some time Atkins had been pressing Gretsch to address the problems he found with hollow-body electrics. Live music, especially rock'n'roll, was being performed at louder volumes on stage, and guitarists playing hollow-body electrics often found themselves plagued by howling feedback when they turned their amplifiers up too high. Feedback is caused by guitar pickups picking up their own sound from the amplifier's loudspeakers, and then feeding it back into the system, creating an unpleasant 'howlround' effect. The increasingly amplified soundwaves move into and around the guitar's body, agitating the strings and top and setting up vibrations that in turn promote more feedback. Players back then considered it a technical nuisance to be avoided – until the mid 1960s, that is, when its musical possibilities began to be exploited.

Atkins and Gretsch decided that one way to diminish this unwanted effect was to block off the f-holes in the guitar's body. So the Country Gentleman appeared in 1957 with what people now generally call 'fake' f-holes. In other words, you can see a visual representation of f-holes on the body, to help the general look of the guitar, but there are no actual holes. At first they were blocked with plastic or wooden infills; later, and when 'fake' f-holes were applied to other Gretsch models (of which more later), they were simply painted on. Atkins told me when we met in 1995 that an early sample guitar, sent to him by Gretsch to check if the idea of closed f-holes was workable, had the filled f-holes covered with sparkly material.

Atkins tried to convince Gretsch that in order to cut feedback – and, more to the point, to enhance his beloved sustain – it would also be useful to make the instrument's hollow body more solid at certain points by adding wooden reinforcement inside. One of the things that encourages a hollowbody guitar to feed back is the way in which the front and back move separately from one another; anything that makes the guitar more sturdy will in theory cut feedback. What Atkins really wanted was a guitar that had a solid wooden section running through the centre of the body from neck to tailpiece – exactly as Gibson did on their ES-335 model that debuted in 1958. Gibson needed this solid centre to mount the bridge and humbucking pickups, but as Gretsch employed a floating bridge and non-height-adjustable humbuckers they had no need for this particular facility. Gretsch were content merely to add twin strengthening braces under the top of the Country Gentleman's body.

> "The Country Gentleman had good tuning pegs, better wood selection, and the body was a little thinner. I started to use it continually on my records." *Chet Atkins*

Atkins, however, was less than content. "I continually tried to get them to make the guitar more solid from the neck down to the end," he remembered. "I wanted more of a sturdy guitar that gave more sustain. Originally the Country Gent did have two braces that went from the end of the guitar to the neck, but they didn't join it, so it still killed off the sustain. They finally made it semi-solid back to the bridge, and had a piece of wood going out to the back, which helped, but it didn't go all the way to the end of the guitar. They never could do that for me."

The other new Chet Atkins model was the red Tennessean 6119, effectively a less fancy one-humbucker version of the 6120, launched in 1958 at $295 (about $100 less than a 6120). Gretsch now had three Chet Atkins models in their line at different price points: relatively low (the $295 Tennessean); middle (the $400 6120); and upper-mid (the $525 Country Gentleman). Naturally they hoped this would secure them a bigger share of the market that Gibson was still dominating.

A number of new features began to appear on the company's guitars, including in 1957 control knobs with Gretsch's classic 'arrow-through-G' design on the top. More noticeable was the latest bridge, the Space Control. No doubt the company reasoned that if they could now make pickups in-house, then they could certainly make their own bridges – enabling them to dispense with Mr Melita's services as well as those of Mr DeArmond's, and thereby gain more control over the production and supply of key components. The Space Control bridge was a Jimmie Webster design, and a lot simpler than Melita's Synchro-Sonic unit. What wouldn't be? It had six wheel-like grooved saddles, each of

TWO CUTAWAYS OR NOT TWO CUTAWAYS?

▾ **1962 Silver Jet in gold**

The 'solidbody' Jet models went twin-cutaway too, in 1961, and a couple of nice examples here give the general idea. The gold sparkle guitar (above) was listed by Gretsch as a variant of the Silver Jet until 1963, alongside options of burgundy, champagne, or tangerine. The guitar also displays the vibrato designed by Burns in London that Gretsch used at the time (this arm – and the tuners – are not original). The later silver-finish Jet (below) is back to a Bigsby wang bar, while its pickups are humbucking Super'Tron types.

▴ **1969 Duo Jet in silver**

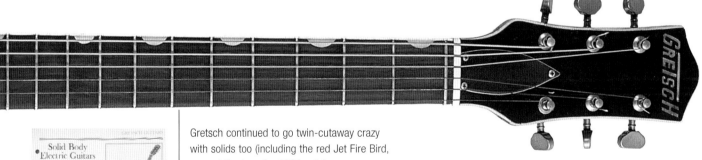

Gretsch continued to go twin-cutaway crazy with solids too (including the red Jet Fire Bird, seen at the top of a 1961 catalogue page, left). Meanwhile, some players were happy to stumble on an older model with the original single cut. One such secondhand treat came Steve Marriott's way, a circa 1960 Chet Atkins Solid Body 6121, seen here with its adoring owner among The Small Faces (above). Later, in summer '67, Steve painted it white, fooling many a logo-spotter into thinking that he'd landed that rare beast, the White Penguin.

which could be positioned as desired along a threaded bar. But intonation adjustment was not possible. Gretsch obviously considered the benefits outweighed such drawbacks, and began to replace the Melita bridge with the Space Control from 1957.

Also new was the 'Neo-Classic' fingerboard, which Gretsch again eulogised in a handy leaflet. "Centuries ago, when string instruments were first built, the early craftsmen discovered that pure ebony offered the best playing performance, and that discovery stands to this very day. As time passed, man decided to decorate these fine playing boards with fancy pearl inlays which were beautiful but in no way helped the playing performance of the board; it only destroyed the wonderful feel only pure satin ebony could give. It is with these proven facts in mind that we introduce the new Gretsch Neo Classic fingerboard – the finest in playing performance and sheer beauty. The beautifully inlaid mother-of-pearl half moons on the bass side of the board are perfect position markers and do not in any way detract from the classic feel which is so essential to perfect performance. Neo Classic construction preserves the full strength of the fingerboard."

How could you refuse? The Neo-Classic markers, also known as 'half moons' or 'thumbnails', first appeared along Gretsch fingerboards during 1958. That same year Gretsch decided to screw a metal plate to the headstock of a number of models. On the plate they put the name of the model and, sometimes, its serial number. Certainly this would help later generations identify some late-1950s and '60s Gretsches.

Also in 1958, Gretsch decided to mark the 75th anniversary of the company's formation and, having already tried the idea with 70th-anniversary accordions in 1953, issued special Anniversary model guitars. They were launched with all the new appointments – one or two Filter'Tron pickups, arrow-through-G knobs, Space Control bridge, Neo-Classic fingerboard – and the 16-inch-wide body was offered in an attractive two-tone green as well as sunburst. Remarkably enough for instruments related to the importance of a solitary year in the company's history, they lasted in the line until 1977 (and were revived in 1993). The relatively low-end Anniversary guitars were in effect stripped-down 6120 models and something of a cheap celebration. "Priced for promotional selling" was the euphemism employed by Gretsch's ad copywriter. But at least the party was a long one.

> Gretsch's stereo guitar gave them an advantage over Gibson for once, with Gibson forced to follow the Gretsch lead, launching their own stereo models a year later.

'Stereo' and 'stereophonic' were magic words in the late 1950s, heralding all that was new and exciting in sound reproduction. During 1956, RCA Victor released the first commercial stereo pre-recorded tapes, followed soon by the first stereo LPs from the major US record labels. Immersed in the potential of electronics and sound, Jimmie Webster put his fertile brain to work on the possibilities of a stereo guitar.

Part of Ray Butts's deal with Gretsch for use of the Filter'Tron pickups involved him as a consultant. He remembered the call. "Jimmie asked me to design a stereo pickup," said Butts. "It was basically quite simple: just take the Filter'Tron and split the windings. Normally you have one winding that covers all six strings. If you cut it in half, you have two separate sets of windings, making three strings independent of the other three. You bring the signals from these windings out separately to separate controls and send them to separate amplifiers. So when you pick the first three strings it comes out of this amp, and the top three strings come out of that amp." That in a nutshell is Gretsch's 'Project-O-Sonic' stereo system, the subject of a Jimmie Webster patent filed in December 1956.

The bridge pickup was located much closer to the neck pickup than usual. The control layout and functions were similar to a normal guitar with two Filter'Trons, but the master volume knob on the cutaway bout was replaced with a three-way switch that selected various combinations of pickups and amps, while the two switches on the upper bout offered independent control of tonal emphasis for each pickup. A special Dual Guitar Cord connected the guitar to a Dual Jack Box, which provided two more sockets to connect to the two amplifiers necessary for stereo reproduction. Gretsch offered their own pair of amps to make a complete stereo outfit. The new Project-O-Sonic stereo system was launched during 1958 as an option available on Country Club and White Falcon models. The Country Club Stereo was priced at $475 in sunburst, $495 natural or green; the White Falcon Stereo was $850. This was $175 more than a regular Falcon, placing it clearly at the top of the Gretsch tree.

WEBSTER'S UNABRIDGED, IN LIVING STEREO

Jimmie Webster recorded an album for RCA Records in December 1958, *Unabridged*, where he made full use of his White Falcon Stereo. Gretsch must have been delighted: the 1959 record amounted to a high-profile demo of their new stereo model. The stereo version was one of the first stereo albums to feature electric guitar. It was produced by Chet Atkins, and was originally recorded at a studio in Nashville. Phil Grant said: "Jimmie made the album with a drummer down there under Chet's tutelage, but I believe there was some kind of technical fault with the recording, and he had to do it over again in New York. They had to have another drummer there, so they got me. My percussion thing was really just to tone up what Jimmie was doing, so that there was something there besides guitar. We had rehearsed quite a bit, so the session went without any hitches."

Gretsch's launch of the stereo guitar gave them an advantage over Gibson for once. Gibson had to follow Gretsch's lead, issuing their own interpretation of the stereo guitar idea in 1959, first with the ES-345 and then the ES-355. Gibson's more straightforward process directed the output of each complete pickup to separate amps.

Gretsch soon modified their first stereo guitar system, and a more complex version began to appear in 1959, previewed by an experimental White Falcon at the company's Guitarama show in Boston in April. Visitors to the Boston demo would have seen a White Falcon with conventional looking Filter'Tron pickups but a more complex control layout. Webster and Butts had once again split the 12 poles of each pickup into two, but had added two more three-way selector switches on the upper bout to give the guitar a total of three control knobs and five selectors. The new pair of switches provided nine combinations of the split pickup sections, and Gretsch calculated that this in combination with the six tonal options provided by the other two selectors gave a grand total of "54 colors and shadings in stereo sound". Presumably the Boston audience would have needed a little time to think about that.

The stereo system was impressive, especially in the hands of its creator. A young Philadelphia-based guitarist, Ross Finley, went to another of the Guitarama promotional shows at a local hotel. Years later he still had a vivid memory of the event. "The White Falcon was a legend," he said. "I'd seen a couple on television but had never seen one up

TWIST MY BIKINI, SAYS PRINCESS

▼ 1961 Corvette

The Corvette model, introduced in 1961, Gretsch's first true solidbody, heavily influenced by Gibson's 'slab'-body twin-cutaway Les Paul Junior of the time. (The control knobs on the Corvette nearby are not the originals.) A year or so later Gretsch revamped the 'vette – as seen in the 1963 catalogue page (opposite) – and again the inspiration came from Gibson, this time recalling the Kalamazoo company's SG Junior.

▲ 1963 Twist

1962 Princess ▸

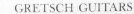

DUO JET
- A STRIKING BLACK BEAUTY
- GOLD PLATED
- EXCLUSIVE GRETSCH TREMOLO

The Duo Jet's striking good looks and superb tone production have made it a stand out performer in every corner of the world. Its compact size allows it to be taken anywhere the guitarist goes.

Double cutaway body with beautiful gleaming black top and mahogany sides and back. 24-karat gold-plated metal parts. Standby switch and exclusive Gretsch vibrato for that tremolo effect.

PX6128 Gretsch Duo Jet Solid Body Electric Guitar .... 164 gns.

THE PERFECT WAY TO MATCH YOUR GUITAR'S COLOR WITH YOUR BAND'S COLOR
The Duo Jet is available on special order with spotlight sparkle finish top in the following popular colors: Silver, Gold, Champagne, Burgundy, Tangerine. The price is the same as for the standard Duo Jet electric guitar.

CORVETTE
- NEW CURVED SHAPE WITH CARVED EDGES
- SOLID MAHOGANY IN CHERRY RED FINISH

Gretsch's more than three-quarters of a century experience: written Guitar Guarantee protects you against defective materials or workmanship.

5

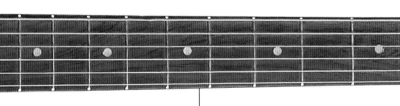

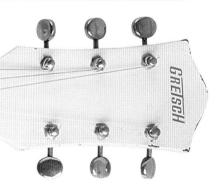

Two whacky variants on the second-style Corvette are seen here. The delightful Twist (main guitar) was intended to cash in on the dance craze and came finished in red or, as here, yellow, with that lovely stripey pickguard. (The bridge is not original.) The Princess (above) was, according to Gretsch, "selectively constructed only for girls". Weirder still was a shortlived Gretsch sideshow, the Bikini (1961 catalogue, left), which had removable necks designed to slide into body 'backs'.

close. So I found out that Jimmie Webster was coming to town with Chet Atkins, on the same bill. Come the day, a few friends and I walk in to this hotel, and I see this guy standing there in the hallway. He's got a dark blue suit on, and he's beckoning to me – I guess we looked like guitar players. So we walked up, he says, 'You fellas looking for the guitar show?' We say yes. He says, 'I'm Jimmie Webster, nice to meet you.' How about that? So we walked into the room, there's the Gretsch catalogue in living colour, every Gretsch you ever saw. The stage was set up: a drum set, two Gretsch amps, and the White Falcon is sitting in the middle. Jimmie Webster came out, pulls this White Falcon up, and they shone a light show on the guitar. As he held it up and the lights hit it, it was like a rainbow. Impressive is a poor word. It's something I'll always remember.

> Some Gretsch hollowbody models began to be made thinner, starting around 1960. The company had discovered with the thinline Country Gentleman model, launched in 1957, that many players preferred the more manageable feel of a slimmer guitar.

"There was something about Jimmie Webster," Finley continued. "He looked like a banker, or a car salesman, anything but this great guitar player. He went almost into a trance before he played: closed his eyes, concentrated for a few seconds, and then produced this incredible sound. I didn't have a very good record-player at the time, everything out of one speaker, and it had never dawned on me that you could take a switch and hit a note and have this sound ping-pong between two speakers. It would start out to his left, over to the right, and back to the left. What a gimmick! Talk about impressed! Years before a wah pedal, and here's this guy doing a trick show."

On the cover of Gretsch's 1959 catalogue the company pictured two White Falcons, one with the new stereo system built in, the other a regular 'mono' example (although surprisingly neither was featured in detail within). This second-type White Falcon Stereo was made available for sale during 1959, while the revised version of the Country Club Stereo appeared in the following year. Gretsch also issued an Anniversary Stereo in 1961 using the original control layout but with split HiLo'Tron single-coil pickups.

But Gretsch had underestimated the conservative nature of many guitar players. Despite Webster's rich imagination and Butts's efficient technical prowess, the stereo Gretsch models did not sell well. Duke Kramer from the company's management team said later that the guitars were just too complicated. "A few players could use the system, but on the Falcon Stereo there were 54 different tone variations, and that got to be a little much for anybody to handle. And in fact there wasn't that much difference between some of the colourings. It never really became too popular."

From around 1959 Gretsch began to fit a 'zero fret' to many guitars. This is an extra fret directly in front of the nut that aims to make the tone of open strings more like those of fretted notes. The fret provides the start of the string's speaking length and creates the string height at this end of the fingerboard, relegating the nut simply to keeping the strings spaced apart. In Gretsch's customarily fanciful marketing hype it was an 'Action-flow fret nut' and remained in use until 1981, and then later on relevant reissues.

The December 1959 pricelist showed a contemporary line-up of no fewer than 15 electric models. There were 11 archtops: Clipper at $175; Anniversary one-pickup $225, two-pickup $310; Chet Atkins Tennessean $325; Sal Salvador $375; Country Club $450 sunburst, $475 natural or Cadillac Green; Chet Atkins Hollow Body 6120 $475; Country Club Stereo $500 sunburst, $525 natural or Cadillac Green; Chet Atkins Country Gentleman $575; White Falcon $750; and White Falcon Stereo $900. There were four semi-solids: the Duo Jet at $310; Jet Fire Bird at $325; Silver Jet $330; and Chet Atkins Solid Body $475.

YOU TOO CAN HAVE A THIN TWIN-CUTAWAY BODY

Come the early 1960s, Gretsch decided on some pretty drastic changes to the shapes and construction of their electric guitars. The body metamorphosis started when some of the hollow models began to be made thinner, starting around 1960. Gretsch had discovered with the thinline Country Gentleman that many players preferred the more manageable feel of a slimmer guitar. So they whittled down the White Falcon from about three to nearer two inches deep, and took a good inch off the two and three-quarter inch deep Country Club, as well as trimming the 6120. The Tennessean was thinned down too, in 1961, given fake f-holes, and the model's existing Filter'Tron humbucking pickup was swapped for two single-coil HiLo'Trons. The transformation would give the $350 model a new popularity during the 1960s.

The Country Gent, 6120 and White Falcon were also entirely transformed in 1961 and 1962, from single to twin-cutaway style. Gibson was as ever the primary inspiration for this decision: since 1958 the Kalamazoo guitar-maker had employed double cutaways to successful effect. Players could more easily reach the higher frets of the fingerboard with this kind of body design, making fuller use of the upper register when soloing. Of course, Gretsch couldn't resist giving the new archtop twin-cutaway body a name: Electrotone. Following the experiment with the Country Gentleman's closed f-holes, this new hollow, sealed Electrotone body generally had 'fake' f-holes stencil-painted on to maintain a reasonably traditional look.

As well as making these sweeping changes to many of the company's models, Gretsch's Jimmie Webster continued to come up with ideas for add-on gadgetry during the early 1960s. He felt they could give Gretsch guitars the edge over the competition. A subsequent outcrop of weird devices began to make the instruments look increasingly complex as the decade progressed.

Many of us regularly use the edge of their picking hand to 'damp' (partially quieten) strings near the bridge. To save us the trouble, Webster came up with a mechanical damper. Gretsch called it a muffler; most people call it a mute. Webster's patent for the mute was filed in February 1962, although it began to appear on guitars around 1960. Depending on the model and period, the mute consists of a single or double pad close to the bridge and under the strings. The pad(s) can be brought into contact with the strings by turning one or two 'dial up' control knobs, also known as 'screw down' knobs, situated either side of the tailpiece – and later changed to 'flip up' lever-action switches. "Eliminates need of the wrist for muffling," said a doubtful Gretsch brochure, "[and] allows complete hand freedom for playing ease." But most players naturally preferred the regular, manual method and ignored Gretsch's shortlived mutes.

A 'standby' switch was added to the control layout of some models from 1961, and it simply turned the guitar's output on or off. The idea was that the instrument could be switched off when not being used but while still plugged into the amplifier. The intention

AN ASTRO JET FOR EVERY SPACE CADET

▲ **1966 Astro Jet**

A third version of the Corvette appeared in 1964, with a two-and-four-tuners headstock style years before Music Man adopted a similar pattern. The two rare colour options (opposite) were made for a California store chain and later nicknamed the 'Silver Duke' and 'Gold Duke'. The Astro Jet (main guitar) was a big, unconventional solidbody that appeared in 1963 and lasted for four years. Take a closer look. There's a nameplate fixed to a body of entirely peculiar proportions. The headstock is similarly skewed, with another take on the two-and-four headstock style. It's mad. No one wanted it. Not surprised.

▲ 1966 Corvette 'Silver Duke'

▲ 1966 Corvette 'Gold Duke'

was not that it could be operated accidentally, so the standby switch was put down by the tailpiece where, it was hoped, it would be out of arm's and harm's way.

Around this time some hollow models began to receive another piece of Webster wildness, the padded back. "For added comfort and playing," ran the catalogue hype, "a springy pad of foam rubber on the guitar back cushions pressure and eliminates fatigue." Gretsch omitted to mention that the pad also conveniently hid the big, ugly control-access plate on the back of the body. Webster's daughter Jennifer remembered going with her father to obtain the padded material from a Long Island supplier of convertible tops and seating covers for cars. Duke Kramer recalled a sort of extended version of the padded back that (thankfully) never made production. "I went to the factory one time and they showed me this padded guitar. The whole guitar was padded! Top, sides, everything. It was a real monster," Kramer said. "I think Jimmie was a little upset when we laughed at him. That one didn't get across."

The Tone Twister was a Webster idea too – his patent was filed in June 1962. It was a small device that clipped on to the 'dead' string area between bridge and tailpiece. Manipulating the small arm attached would enable the brave player to induce vibrato effects. It also had the undesirable ability to achieve startling string-breaking effects, which rather limited its popularity.

IT'S JUST MY SLANTED FRETS, NURSE

T-Zone Tempered Treble was the grand name given to Jimmie Webster's slanted frets idea. He was down at the patent office again in February 1962 for this one. Quality-control man Dan Duffy recalled: "Jimmie would tell us that when you tune a piano – remember he was a piano player and had his own piano-tuning business – you always tune the upper register a little sharper than the bass. That's the way the human ear hears."

And so for their Tempered Treble, Gretsch would slant the frets by one degree from the 12th fret and above, resulting in the treble strings being slightly sharpened. The White Falcon and Viking models that bore this questionable modification from 1964 were given offset dot markers in the slanted zone. "You will never notice the slight degree in your fingering but you will notice a beautiful change in your treble range," insisted Gretsch.

Next came the Floating Sound Unit, in 1966 (patent filed August 1965), another idea that Webster pulled from his piano-tuning bag. Strings are threaded through a three-bar frame that sits between bridge and mute. Fixed to the underside of the frame is a tuning fork that passes downwards through a hole in the top of the body and makes contact with the guitar's back. The theory was that this would improve sustain, but mostly the unit just rattled around and ruined any attempts to intonate the guitar accurately. Many Floating Sound Units have subsequently been removed by exasperated guitarists. Webster himself tended to use a variety that left the low E-string free, which he would replace with a bass E, an octave below the regular type. In a Gretsch leaflet this is called the 'Octo-Bass' scheme. Chet Atkins said: "Jimmie's tuning-fork idea was supposed to make the guitar sustain, but the bass strings didn't have any balls. I had them make me a tuning fork that just was on the first four strings, but I never did utilise it."

Atkins went on to explain the reasoning behind Webster's 1960s gizmos. "Jimmie said to me, 'You've got to give them something different all the time. It's like a car, you've got to come up with something new, they want new features.' And I guess he was right. He was a hell of a salesman. But I never liked them all." And the Gretsch view? Duke Kramer: "Some of Jimmie's ideas were good, some were bad. The padded back was OK, the Tempered Treble was a little far fetched, and the Floating Sound Unit was an absolute pain in the neck." Dan Duffy: "I didn't always agree with Jimmie, but you had to train yourself to be commercially minded. You couldn't go into the factory every day and be a jazz guitar player, you had to go in there and be a businessman. Those guitars had to play right, and get the hell out the door so the money came in. That's what it was all about."

The solidbody line also went twin-cutaway from 1961, although very few Chet Atkins Solid Body models were made in this style, and a twin-winged White Penguin would be an even rarer find than the single-cutaway version. Soon after Gretsch changed the solids to the double-cutaway style, they also replaced the Bigsby vibrato tailpieces with British Burns-designed units, probably because of supply irregularities from Bigsby. Quite why Gretsch should choose the product of a small maker from the UK is a mystery – although it's fun to speculate that if Jimmie Webster and Jim Burns had met at a trade show they would surely have had a great time discussing bizarre guitar gadgetry. Whatever the reason, Gretsch carried on using the Burns vibratos on their solid lines into the mid 1960s.

During the early part of the 1960s Gretsch toyed with a number of oddball solidbody designs. Local guitarist Charles Savona brought the idea for the Bikini model to the company. He had in mind a hinged, folding body 'back' into which one could slide interchangeable guitar and bass necks. The body 'backs' would be in both single and double-neck styles, and the result was intended to be a versatile, portable guitar. Or so Savona assured them. However, Dan Duffy remembered something of a struggle bringing the Bikini to production. "People at the factory worked diligently to design the 'butterfly' backs so that the slide-in track would work right. It was a great idea, but in my estimation it wasn't really engineered correctly."

A Bikini neck and back was catalogued at $175, bass neck and back $195, and a double back with guitar and bass necks $355. Single backs could be bought separately for $25, double backs for $35. Bill Hagner, who became factory manager at Gretsch in 1961, also recalled the Bikini causing some suffering at the workbenches. "You talk about a hard guitar to make," he laughed. "Forget about it! Headache! To get that thing on correctly and sliding up and down – it was awful. We didn't make that many of the Bikini, thank god."

In 1961 Gretsch needed a cheaper solidbody to compete with Gibson's $155 Les Paul Junior and came up with the $139.50 Corvette, their cheapest solid. This was Gretsch's first true solidbody guitar, without the body 'pockets' of earlier models. It came with a HiLo'Tron single-coil pickup, and started life with a simple 'slab' body similar to the old Junior's, but subsequently gained bevelled-edge contours, influenced by Gibson's new SG design.

An interesting variation on that later contoured Corvette was the colourful Princess model of 1962. "For the first time in guitar manufacturing history an instrument has been selectively constructed only for girls," ran Gretsch's ad. "This is the unique adaptable Gretsch Princess Guitar, engineered with identical Gretsch precision to meet the needs

> "For added comfort and playing, a springy pad of foam rubber on the guitar back cushions pressure and eliminates fatigue." *Gretsch catalogue, early 1960s*

A LITTLE BIT GRETSCH

▲ 1966 12-String

▲ 1967 Monkees

1967 Viking ▸

Debuting on American television in September 1966, The Monkees were instantly successful ... and soon proved their musical worth as they began to play on their own records. Mike Nesmith (above) was often seen with the Gretsch 12-string that the company gave to the group along with other instruments aimed at publicising the Gretsch name (and trumpeted in a trade ad, left). The 12-String became a production item (opposite, top) as did a shortlived Monkees model (main guitar). At the same time Gretsch added a high-end electric to its guitar line, the Viking (above).

and standards of young women all over the world." Gretsch had simply finished the Corvette in special pastel colour combinations designed to appeal to the delicate female sensibility. The boys at Gretsch offered White body with Grape pickguard, Blue body with White pickguard, Pink body with White pickguard, or White body with Gold pickguard. The girls failed to respond to such charms, however, and the Princess retired from public view.

Another opportunist variant of the 1962 Corvette was Gretsch's Twist model. Chubby Checker's 'The Twist' 45 had topped the US chart for the second time, in January, and set off the twist dance fad. "You follow a trend," explained Duke Kramer. "The twist dance was an absolute craze, everyone was doing the twist. What better than to bring out a Twist guitar?" This coloured Corvette had a pickguard bearing a twisting red and white 'peppermint' design. Of course, the Twist did not last long.

Gretsch's pricelist of September 1962 sums up a line of 19 electrics. There were 12 archtops: the Clipper at $189; Anniversary one-pickup at $225, two-pickup $295; Chet Atkins Tennessean $350; Sal Salvador $375; Anniversary Stereo $375; Chet Atkins Hollow Body 6120 $495; Country Club $495; Country Club Stereo $550; Chet Atkins Country Gentleman $595; White Falcon $800; and White Falcon Stereo $1,000. There were seven solids: the Corvette (one-pickup) at $148, or with vibrato $185; Twist at $149, or with vibrato $189; Princess $169; Duo Jet $350; Jet Fire Bird $350; Silver Jet $350; and Chet Atkins Solid Body $425.

The last of Gretsch's new early-1960s solidbodys was the $295 Astro-Jet, which appeared around 1963. "Hand-carved edges highlight its unusual body design," said the catalogue. When Gretsch, no strangers themselves in the land of weird, said something was 'unusual' you just knew it had to be truly outlandish. The Astro-Jet was indeed a very strange looking guitar, almost as if it had been left out too long on a hot Brooklyn summer day and melted into several disfigured lumps. Salvador Dali might have painted an electric guitar that looked like this. It was big, too, the body measuring 16 inches across, some three inches wider than most Gretsch solids.

> "Chet Atkins' picking has inspired so many guitarists throughout the world, myself included – but I didn't have enough fingers at the time."
> *George Harrison*

The Astro-Jet featured Gretsch's new Super'Tron humbucking pickup, visually characterised by the absence of polepieces; instead it has two long, bar-shaped, laminated poles on the top. The intention was a 'hotter' humbucker than the regular Filter'Tron, but the Super was never as popular. As for the peculiar Astro-Jet, Duke Kramer recalled it as "an effort to bring out something that would compete with Fender but not look like Fender. It was a heavy guitar, an awkward shape. It didn't play too bad but it just didn't catch the imagination of the players. I don't know who was responsible for the design, but I suppose I can push it on to Jimmie Webster".

In 1964 along came the Viking, Gretsch's first new archtop electric since the Chet Atkins Tennessean model six years earlier. At $650 the 17-inch-body Viking was second only to the $850 White Falcon in price, and with all the paraphernalia of the period – mutes, T-Zone frets, padded back, telescopic vibrato arm and all – could almost be considered as a mono Falcon for those who didn't fancy a white guitar with a winged headstock. The Cadillac Green-finished Viking was, like the sunburst variety, pitched at $650, while a natural no-paint-at-all job would, perversely as ever, cost the 1960s guitarist an extra $25.

In Liverpool, England, in August 1960 a fledgling group called The Beatles set out to start a run of no fewer than 48 nights at the Indra club in Hamburg, their first visit to this lively port city in northern Germany. Seventeen-year-old guitarist George Harrison took with him his Futurama, a cheap Czech-made solidbody electric guitar. But Harrison had decided he needed something better. After all, his co-guitarist in the group, John Lennon, had recently bought a new Rickenbacker 325, which was exactly what most British guitarists wanted but few possessed – an American guitar. "I might manage a red Fender Stratocaster with gold plating … but the one I want is the Gretsch," he wrote to a friend in October. The following summer he got lucky.

"We started making a bit of money," Harrison later told *Guitar Player*, "because I saved up £75, and I saw an ad in the paper in Liverpool, and there was a guy selling his guitar." It turned out to be a sailor who had purchased a Gretsch Duo Jet in the US and brought it back to England. "It was my first real American guitar," Harrison recalled, "and I'll tell you, it was secondhand, but I polished that thing. I was so proud to own that." Over the next few years The Beatles began their dramatic rise to fame, and Harrison continued to use his beloved 1957 Duo Jet – with its DeArmond pickups, hump-block markers, and arrow-through-G knobs – on the group's early gigs and recordings.

GEORGE, CHET, AND A MUTUAL FRIEND

Buoyed up by his group's great success in Britain, Harrison bought a new Gretsch Country Gentleman around April 1963 at the Sound City store in central London. Andy Babiuk reports in his definitive book, *Beatles Gear*, that Harrison paid £264 for the guitar – the equivalent of about $740 at the time, and in today's money some £3,300 ($5,500).

No doubt Harrison, a Chet Atkins fan, was pleased to own a guitar named for his hero. Asked to provide a sleevenote for Chet's 1966 Lennon-McCartney covers album *Picks On the Beatles*, Harrison wrote: "I have appreciated Chet Atkins as a musician since long before the tracks on this album were written; in fact, since I was the ripe young age of 17. Since then I have lost count of the number of Chet's albums I have acquired, but I have not been disappointed with any of them.

"For me, the great thing about Mr. Atkins is not the fact that he is capable of playing almost every type of music, but the conviction in the way he does it. … 'I'll Cry Instead', 'She's A Woman' and 'Can't Buy Me Love', having a country feeling about them, lend themselves perfectly to Chet's own style of picking, which has inspired so many guitarists throughout the world (myself included, but I didn't have enough fingers at the time). All the other tracks have Chet adding harmonies and harmonics in the least expected places, bringing out that crystal-clear sound of the guitar to his audience's benefit."

A few weeks after buying his new twin-cutaway Country Gent, Harrison used it to record 'She Loves You'. This Gent had the 'screw down' mute knobs either side of the tailpiece, but in October Harrison acquired a replacement after the first guitar became damaged; this new Gent had the 'flip up' mute switches, and quickly became his prime instrument. (Like most players, Harrison completely avoided the mutes, of course.) That second Gent was one of the guitars most associated with the Beatle until it was destroyed in an accident at the end of 1965. Crucially, it was the guitar Harrison was seen with in February 1964 when the group played their first concerts in the United States and made appearances on the *Ed Sullivan* TV show. By that time he'd indulged his passion for

SIX PLUS ONE EQUALS VAN EPS

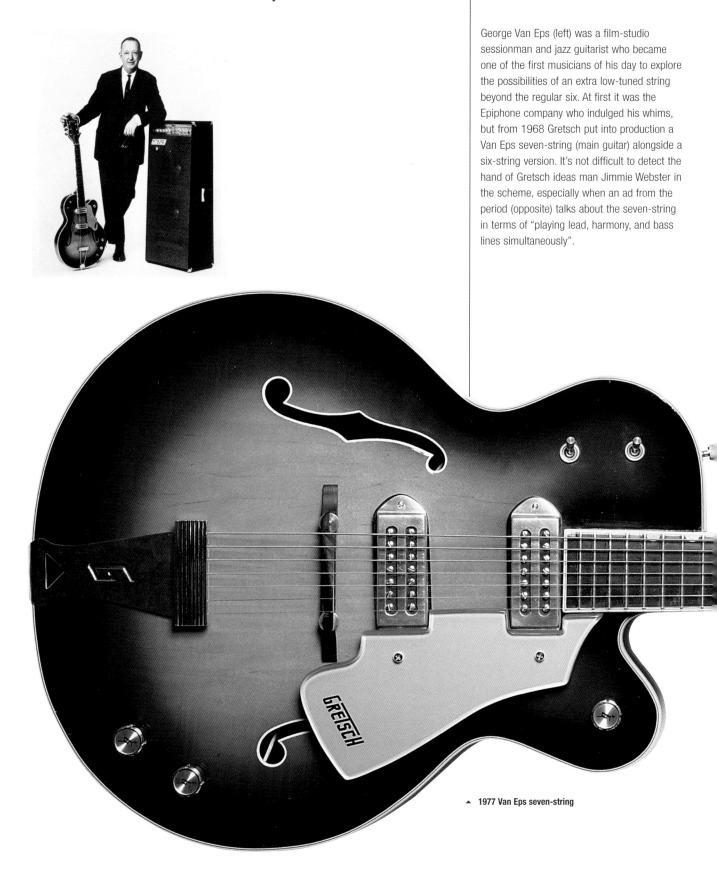

George Van Eps (left) was a film-studio sessionman and jazz guitarist who became one of the first musicians of his day to explore the possibilities of an extra low-tuned string beyond the regular six. At first it was the Epiphone company who indulged his whims, but from 1968 Gretsch put into production a Van Eps seven-string (main guitar) alongside a six-string version. It's not difficult to detect the hand of Gretsch ideas man Jimmie Webster in the scheme, especially when an ad from the period (opposite) talks about the seven-string in terms of "playing lead, harmony, and bass lines simultaneously".

▲ **1977 Van Eps seven-string**

1968 Rally ▶

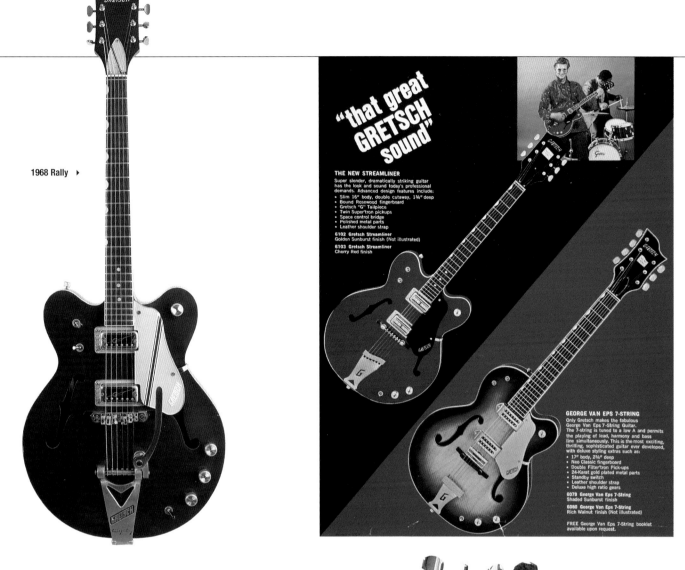

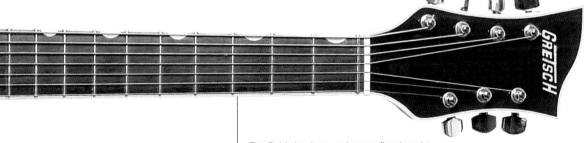

The Baldwin piano and organ firm bought
Gretsch in 1967. It must have seemed like a
good idea at the time but the soul of the victim
soon seemed to fade. The first new Gretsch
after Baldwin took over was the Rally (above
left), a colourful enough contender, but lacking
any real sparkle. (The bridge on this one is not
original.) It had a built-in treble booster – but
already sported trebly HiLo'Tron pickups. An
old name was revived for another 'new' model
in 1968, the Streamliner (ad, above right). Two
years later production shifted from the factory
Gretsch had opened in 1916 in Brooklyn, New
York City, to a new plant in Booneville, Kansas.

Gretsch still further, acquiring over the 1963/64 new year a two-pickup single-cutaway Tennessean, which he used in the studio and for live shows in '64 and, especially, in '65 (as seen in the *Help!* movie).

Following on from their domination in Britain, The Beatles had a devastating effect on American youth; hundreds of bands were formed across the country in the wake of the *Sullivan* shows and many of them sought the guitars played by the Liverpudlian invaders. One such was David Crosby of the fledgling Byrds, who bought a Tennessean. Bandmate Roger McGuinn also used that guitar, as he explained years later. "Everyone says it was David's Gretsch, but it was *our* Gretsch. I actually played that for the lead on 'Have You Seen Her Face' and other tracks on our first album, *Mr Tambourine Man*."

Many more 1960s pickers tried Gretsch guitars in the wake of The Beatles' success and Harrison's example. Brian Jones of the Stones used a Gretsch Anniversary on stage from late 1963 into the following year. Steve Marriott of The Small Faces was one of the few opting for a Chet Solid Body, which he later painted white.

Chris Britton's Country Gent graced many a Troggs track, including that stirring opening to 'Wild Thing'. Eric Clapton briefly tried a double-cut 6120 while in The Yardbirds, but gave up after finding it "too complicated". Neil Young played a single-cut 6120 to great effect in his first notable group, Buffalo Springfield – and would go on to give Gretsch a new prominence in the following decade. Lou Reed almost got a Gent in tune on the early Velvet Underground records.

Harrison was well aware of the impact that he and his group had on instrument sales. "I read somewhere that after The Beatles appeared on [the *Sullivan* shows] Gretsch sold 20,000 guitars a week, or something like that," he said later. "I mean, we would have had shares in Fender, Vox, Gretsch and everything, but we didn't know."

ALMOST A GEORGE HARRISON MODEL

Gretsch made some efforts to capitalise further on the fact that the lead guitarist in the most famous group in the world was actively and visibly playing their instruments. Of course, The Beatles were caught in a whirlwind of success, and offers for marketing opportunities were surfacing from every entrepreneur who wanted to sell a Beatles wig or a plastic guitar off the back of the fab four's success. But Gretsch's Jimmie Webster did in fact make a promotional visit to Britain in April 1964 and had every intention of meeting with George while he was over. "There was supposed to be a meeting," recalled Webster's daughter Jennifer, "but it didn't happen. I don't think my father really cared that much personally," she laughs, "but he was willing to explore the idea of developing a guitar with him. And business had picked up when George used a Gretsch. My father was raving about that: 'Keep doing it, keep doing it,' he'd say, 'that's what we need!'"

It seems likely that if Webster had met Harrison they would have discussed a Harrison model that Gretsch was keen to produce. Later, in October, the company had a custom-made 12-string guitar delivered to Harrison during a British tour. The one-off guitar was something like a black single-cut Tennessean, but with real f-holes, Super'Tron pickups, no Bigsby, and, of course, 12 strings. It also had a somewhat presumptuous plate on the headstock reading "George Harrison Model". But Harrison didn't care for the guitar – after all, he had a fine Rickenbacker 12-string – and soon gave it away to a musician friend. Presumably Gretsch too quickly forgot about the idea.

The Beatles and the groups who came in their wake triggered a boom in guitar popularity during the middle 1960s, and the US industry hit a peak in 1965 with sales of around a million and a half instruments. A strong link to the biggest group of the time – even without any official partnership – certainly did a company like Gretsch little harm. Thanks to Harrison and his highly visible Country Gent and Tennessean, business was good and the orders came flying in. "The guitar is truly the sound of the day," a jubilant Jimmie Webster told a trade gathering at the time.

Some organisational changes became necessary at Gretsch's headquarters in New York City to deal with this exceptional shift in the balance of their trade. One insider's estimate is that Gretsch had around 5,000 orders for electric guitars stacking up at the time, and that a customer wanting one of the most popular models, such as the Country Gentleman, might have to wait over a year. Something had to change. It was announced in October 1965 that the drum department would move out of the Brooklyn factory to another location a few blocks away, on South 5th Street, and many of the wholesaling operations were either stopped or moved to the Chicago office. All this was to allow the whole of the seventh floor to be turned over to guitar making.

Quality controller Dan Duffy, who by now had taken on more people such as Fred Rodriguez to cope with the increased demands on his department, remembered the changes well. "The transformation was amazing, totally mind boggling," he said. "The changes in that factory during the ten years since I started in 1956 were amazing. You have to picture a company back in the 1950s trying to make 12 guitars a day, and possibly only getting out eight. In '66 we'd be aiming for 75, and some days we'd make 100 and more. We had racks made to hold 20 guitars, you'd see Country Gents, Anniversary models, White Falcons all lined up, 20 to a rack, being moved throughout the factory. It was the most spectacular experience in my life."

NOT ENOUGH MONKEE BUSINESS

Another kind of pop experience awaited Gretsch. In the mid 1960s an American production company, Screen Gems, manufactured The Monkees by hiring four actors and singers. The group debuted in September 1966 on US TV in a series about the group's zany escapades, openly exploiting the success of The Beatles and in particular the style of the *Hard Day's Night* movie.

After the failure of the 'signature' Beatles guitar, perhaps Gretsch thought that a Monkees-endorsed model would be the next best thing. Phil Grant took a hardline musician's view. "Fred Gretsch Jr, Jimmie Webster and I went to a place in New York and watched some Monkees footage – they wanted us to sponsor the group with guitars and drums. I wasn't very enthusiastic about it. I've found that endorsements are only good if people look up to the fellow who's endorsing, if he's a real musician. The Monkees were a bunch of idiots: they were singers, and their playing was absolutely incidental to their act. So I said I'm not for it because they're not musicians, it's an insult to Chet Atkins and all the good drummers to say that these guys are Gretsch people. They were lousy musicians."

Grant was out-voted, and in 1966 Gretsch supplied instruments to the group, including two of the company's new 12-string guitars, one in natural and another in an unusual white finish, two basses, and a drum set. The group's Mike Nesmith had earlier converted a

OLD GUITARS FOR NEW MUSIC

▲ 1972 Roc Jet

▲ 1972 Super Chet

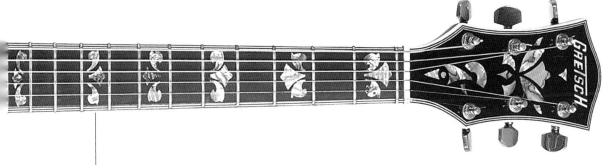

A new Booneville-factory model was the large, ornate Super Chet (main guitar), unusually with controls on the edge of the pickguard (the bank of eight switches was a later addition by owner Chet Atkins). Meanwhile, some players had started to look for 'vintage' guitars, believing that current guitar-making skills had dimmed. The Roc Jet (opposite) was a reaction to Gibson's recent re-introduction of the old-style single-cut Les Paul. In '71 Pete Townshend (top) urges on a circa-1958 Chet 6120, while Neil Young is pictured (right) in '74 with a circa-1960 White Falcon Stereo.

standard Gretsch six-string to a 12, and so may well have been the most excited Monkee about the association. In one TV episode he was even seen with a Tennessean-style 12-string. Later, he switched to Gibson, Micky Dolenz to Slingerland drums, and Peter Tork to a Guild bass. Nesmith's prized Gretsch was later stolen, and eventually the revived company would make him a replica in 1997 for use on a Monkees reunion album.

It was during 1966 that Gretsch put a Monkees model on to the market, a red twin-cutaway thinline six-string emblazoned with Monkees guitar-shaped logos on truss-rod cover and pickguard. The group appeared in Gretsch ads at the time. "But we got letters from customers," remembered Dan Duffy, "and they'd say, 'Please send me a plain Gretsch pickguard and rod shield cover.' They didn't want the association of The Monkees on the guitar! We thought it was the best thing on the guitar, so attractive, and no one wanted it. They didn't want their guitar to be associated with The Monkees, maybe because they knew that the group didn't really play." The model never appeared in an official catalogue or pricelist, and did not last long in the line.

Shockwaves had been sent through the guitar manufacturing industry in 1965 when Fender was sold to the Columbia Broadcasting System corporation for $13million. It was by far and away the biggest sum ever paid for an instrument business, and other large companies began to look at the potential of the "expanding leisure-time market", as Fender's purchaser described it.

D H Baldwin, an Ohio-based musical instrument company specialising in the manufacture of pianos and organs, wanted to buy a guitar-making operation. In 1965 they had bid unsuccessfully for Fender. They then bought the Burns guitar company of England for £250,000, applying the Baldwin brandname to many existing Burns models. Baldwin's 1966 Annual Report described a rosy picture: for the first time in the company's long history, overall sales exceeded $40million, and for the fifth year sales and profits were up. There had been a decline in keyboard instrument sales, but "since guitars and amplifiers were introduced in the latter part of 1965, there were substantial increases over the figures of the previous year". Baldwin decided they could benefit further with a guitar brandname that had an existing high profile in the US – and turned their attention to Gretsch. Every year, Duke Kramer and Phil Grant, the Gretsch vice-presidents based in Chicago and New York respectively, would go to dinner with Fred Gretsch Jr on their return from the music trade fair in Frankfurt, Germany. Early in 1967, the dinner date with their 62-year-old boss came around.

"We were back from a very successful fair," said Kramer, "and Fred drops this bomb on us that he was selling the company to Baldwin. It was a real shake-up." Grant recalled: "He mixed us a stiff drink each, and said, 'I have some news for you. I'm selling the company to Baldwin.' Well, we didn't know how to take it – and there was nothing much you could do about it."

Dick Harrison was Baldwin's treasurer at the time of the acquisition (later vice-president and then chief executive officer). He was involved in the negotiation and completion of the

> "We got letters from Gretsch Monkee customers and they'd say, 'Please send me a plain Gretsch pickguard.' They didn't want the association of The Monkees on the guitar! We thought it was the best thing, and no one wanted it." *Dan Duffy, Gretsch*

transaction, reporting to Baldwin's top man Morley Thompson who spearheaded the deal. Harrison told me about Fred Gretsch's reasons for selling. "I don't believe he had any offspring who were interested in pursuing the company; he had a young daughter, I believe, and that was all. I'm sure that he knew he had a company in an industry that was growing, and if he was ever going to diversify it would be a smart time to do that. I'm sure that's why he did it, and that's what he told me. Of course, we were dealing with a man who's giving up everything he owns in the way of a company, and naturally he wants to be careful how he does it. But they were good negotiations with no major problems."

NOW THE BOSS IS BALDWIN

The sale was completed on July 31st 1967, and *The Music Trades* reported that "10,000 shares of Baldwin common stock and an undisclosed sum of cash" were involved. Some observers have since suggested an unofficial figure of $4million. The report continued: "A new Baldwin subsidiary, organized to acquire these assets, will have Fred Gretsch as president. No change in the management of Gretsch is contemplated. … Gretsch's sales in 1966 were in excess of $6million. The acquisition of Gretsch will expand Baldwin's business in the guitar field and will put Baldwin in the drum and band instrument business."

It wasn't only the brandname and products that Baldwin considered valuable. They also recognised the worth of the most important name still associated with Gretsch guitars – Chet Atkins – and ensured that this property remained secure.

"I was important to that sale," Atkins told me. "Mr Gretsch came to me, said he was gonna sell to Baldwin, and asked me if I would sign a contract for so many years. I said, 'Why don't I get some stock?' And he wouldn't do it. I was real busy at the time, and I didn't have an attorney or anything, so I went ahead and signed it." It was also around this time that the 6120 had a switch of identity. The official model name was changed from Chet Atkins Hollow Body to the more friendly Chet Atkins Nashville. The guitar itself stayed the same.

> "Baldwin was the greatest manufacturer of organs and pianos, but they tried to put their men into the guitar business, and it wasn't right." *Bill Hagner, Gretsch*

Meanwhile, Gretsch personnel began to overcome their initial surprise at the takeover and looked to a new future. Factory manager Bill Hagner said there were changes. "The Baldwin company were the greatest manufacturing company of organs and pianos, but they tried to put their men into the guitar and drum business, and it wasn't the right thing to do. They had their own so-called engineers and so-called chemists and so-called this and that, and they wanted to incorporate their methods that they used in making pianos and organs. They said: 'Now we're going to do it this way,' and I would say, 'Wait a minute, we made that mistake 20 years ago.'"

Phil Grant reflected on Fred Gretsch Jr's motives for selling, and concluded: "I can't blame Fred, looking back on it now. But the usual thing happened: a company was bought up and the president promises nothing's going to change, your jobs are all secure, don't worry." Grant laughed: "And your cheque's in the mail! Anyway … I went along with it, and after a while you could see that things weren't going to be the way that you hoped they would be. Baldwin would press a button, say, 'Let's do it this way,' and anybody's personal feelings never entered into their decisions at all."

1980 White Falcon Stereo ▶

1975 White Falcon ▶

▲ 1975 Country Roc

PAST GLORIES STILL TO COME

Gradually during the 1970s Gretsch began to notice new players using their older guitars. For example, here's AC/DC's Malcolm Young (above, left) in '76 with his modified double-cut 60s Jet Firebird. Gretsch's Country Roc (main guitar) was added to the line in 1974, recalling the 50s Round Up, including a 'G-brand' on the body front. But the circuitry and Super'Trons were more contemporary. Another visit back to the past came the same year with the reintroduction of the single-cutaway White Falcon (opposite, top; and on 1975 catalogue cover, far left), but again mostly featuring contemporary hardware rather than as a period-accurate reissue. Nonetheless, the return to the single cutaway does in effect mark it as the first official 'retro' Gretsch – of which much more was to come. Meanwhile the double-cut Falcon continued, including the still multi-controlled Stereo version (opposite).

Baldwin was disappointed with the business results of the merger. "When you put two companies together you like to believe that one plus one equals three," said Dick Harrison. "If you have a sales force out there that would be capable of selling Gretsch guitars in addition to Baldwin pianos, that would have represented some synergy. In other words you would come out better by having done it. But the products were so different, and we felt that it would have been a great mistake to put the Gretsch guitar in the hands of our Baldwin sales people, so we never did that. Another example of synergy would have been if our factories that make pianos, primarily woodworking operations, could make guitars. Again, they're so different that that didn't come about.

"Gretsch did well for a while," concluded Harrison, "but then the industry turned down and of course that hurt us. I would say that it really wasn't a financial success for us. And that certainly wasn't the fault of anybody from Gretsch; that was as much the industry's fault and our fault as anything else." Baldwin had begun to diversify away from their original core of music and into financial services, including banking and insurance. The company's Annual Report for 1969 noted a 12 percent drop in Gretsch sales, conveniently attributing over half the fall to a three-month strike that began in October 1969.

FROM BROOKLYN TO BOONEVILLE

By the following year, plans were underway to move the Gretsch factory out of its 54-year-old home in Brooklyn to a site in Booneville, Arkansas, well over 1,000 miles away, where Baldwin already operated a number of factories and enjoyed the fruits of a cheaper and more amenable workforce. Of course, the move did not please the already disgruntled workers, and very few made the move south-west in September 1970.

The Gretsch sales office had been moved from the Brooklyn building to the Chicago office in August 1969, and in May 1972 to Baldwin's HQ in Cincinnati, Ohio. This meant that by the early 1970s Gretsch had severed the last connection with their longstanding HQ at 60 Broadway, Brooklyn.

One of the few who relocated to the Booneville site was factory manager Bill Hagner. "I moved everything down and set it up, and I taught the new people what to do and how to do it. That lasted several years. The factory was a big converted barn up on top of the mountain about five miles out of a small town of 3,000 people. You had to take people off the farms and try to teach them how to work. When you're used to New York, well … . You move down there and they'd be polishing a guitar for four hours instead of a half hour." Hagner lasted at Booneville until 1972 when he was moved to Baldwin's Ohio offices to work with the sales force. Some of the old names remained: Fred Gretsch Jr had become a Baldwin board member in December 1967; Duke Kramer went to Cincinnati in 1972 as Gretsch's general sales manager. Dan Duffy left in 1970, at first going back to full-time playing and teaching, and then on to positions in various instrument companies, while Phil Grant left in 1972 to set up a grocery business in Vermont.

Jimmie Webster made some Guitarama-style appearances for Gretsch after the sale to Baldwin, but gradually drifted away from the guitar company that he had done so much to establish. Webster died in 1978 at the age of 69. Chet Atkins, who switched to a deal with the Gibson company in the 1980s, offered me a concise recollection of the Gretsch/Baldwin set-up. "They just couldn't build Gretsch guitars at Booneville. I complained, and they hired a man called Dean Porter. He moved to Arkansas and got the guitars so they would play. But the quality never was like it was in Brooklyn." Atkins himself played great guitar, as ever, for the rest of his life. He died in 2001.

Just before the Baldwin buy-out, Gretsch's pricelist of November 1966 detailed 15 electrics in the line. There were 11 archtops: the Clipper at $200; Anniversary one-pickup $245, two-pickup $300; Chet Atkins Tennessean $400; Country Club $475 sunburst, $500 natural; Chet Atkins Hollow Body 6120 $500; 12-String $500; Chet Atkins Country Gentleman $650; Viking $675 sunburst or Cadillac Green, $700 natural; White Falcon $900; and White Falcon Stereo $1,000. There were four solids: the Corvette (two-pickup) $265; Astro-Jet $350; Duo Jet $375 (including colour sparkle options); and Jet Fire Bird $375.

The first catalogue issued after Baldwin took over in 1967 highlighted the return of Bigsby vibratos to the solidbody models after the dalliance with Burns, as well as the first new Gretsch model of the Baldwin era, the $395 Rally. This was a twin-cutaway thinline archtop with 16-inch-wide body, unusual in that it featured a built-in active treble-boost circuit, which was also added to the Corvette at this time. The circuit may have been derived from Baldwin's Burns connection, as the UK company had pioneered active circuitry in the early 1960s. Quite why Gretsch wanted to boost the treble of a guitar already equipped with trebly HiLo'Tron single-coil pickups is unclear.

Definitely borrowed from Baldwin's Burns-originated guitars was the 'gear box' method of truss-rod adjustment, accessed through the back of the body at the neck heel. Gretsch began to incorporate this on their instruments during the early 1970s, coincidentally following the cessation of Baldwin/Burns instrument production in Britain. Under Baldwin, Gretsch also decided that the time was right to allow air into their 'sealed' archtops by reviving real, open f-holes on the bodies from about 1972.

Before production moved in 1970 from Brooklyn to Booneville there was a period when Gretsch made a number of limited-run instruments for various retailers, players, teachers and so on. Not that Gretsch had ever been shy of custom work, most famously exemplified by that handful of odd-shaped solids made for Bo Diddley around 1960.

An insider explained: "Gretsch was always small enough to be flexible, and always tried to fill small niches in the business. That's why nobody can nail down what Gretsch did on a particular model, because maybe ten percent of our business was custom guitars. If someone wanted a pink guitar with blue stripes, we made it. If somebody wanted a guitar with a narrow neck at the nut, we made it. It cost the customer extra money, but we were small enough to be able to do that sort of thing."

Small-order batches in the 1960s included specially modified models for Gretsch dealers such as Sam Ash (Anniversary-style with cat's-eye shape soundholes), Sam Goody (twin-cutaway archtop with 'G' soundholes), and Sherman Clay (gold- and silver-finish Corvettes, later nicknamed 'Silver Duke' and 'Gold Duke'). Our insider continued: "Dealers liked the idea of an exclusive instrument because they could point to it and say 'no one else has it', and they could charge a certain amount of dollars and know that

> "Maybe ten percent of our business was custom guitars. If someone wanted a pink guitar with blue stripes, then we made it. It cost the customer extra money, but we were small enough to be able to do that sort of thing." *Gretsch worker, late 1960s*

THE END OF GRETSCH – FOR NOW

▲ 1979 Beast BST-1000

▲ 1977 Super Axe

▲ 1978 TK300

1978 Committee ▶

That great Gretsch sound!

A NEW GRETSCH GREAT!

THE ATKINS SUPER AXE

GRETSCH

The Baldwin-owned Gretsch operation was running out of steam, and while the guitars here weren't out of keeping with contemporary trends, they didn't exactly scream "Buy me!" The TK300 (main guitar) had some Fender influence (yet none of that brand's effortless style), with bolt-on neck and six-tuners-on-one-side headstock, and cheap Japanese humbuckers that made for a raucous experience. Another bolt-on model introduced in the late 1970s was the Beast (left, top). The Committee (above left, and on 1978 catalogue cover) followed a trend for through-neck construction, with body 'wings' added to an instrument-length neck, believed to enhance sustain. The latest Chet-endorsed model came in '77, the effects-laden solidbody Super Axe (opposite). In the ad (left) Chet described the Axe as "the ultimate guitar for the rock musican" but very few agreed with him.

nobody could quote a cheaper price." Special small-run 'signature' guitars were also made, including a limited number for New York-based player/teacher/store-owner Ronny Lee, as well as some six and seven-string models named for guitarist George Van Eps, the seven-string version of which remained in the catalogue for ten years.

Van Eps had become well known for big-band work from the 1930s, and after World War II had moved to the West Coast and successfully concentrated on film-studio sessions. During the late 1930s the Epiphone company built him a custom guitar based on his unusual requirement for a seven-string model, adding a low-A below the existing E-string. (This was over 40 years before Steve Vai came up with a similar idea, one that would be developed by late-1990s metal bands such as Korn.) Van Eps once explained that he wanted the additional low A-string because of his love of deep basslines, and because he approached the guitar as "a complete instrument within itself", almost as if it were a mini-orchestra. Gretsch produced Van Eps single-cutaway models from 1968, in six-string ($575) as well as seven-string ($675) versions, each with a 17-inch-wide body. They underline again the company's flexible approach that enabled it to manufacture small numbers of limited-appeal instruments – even if it did mean tooling-up for the unique 14-pole humbuckers necessary for the seven-string.

> George Van Eps wanted a special seven-string Gretsch because of his love of deep basslines and his view of the guitar as "a complete instrument within itself".

Of course, Gretsch was still keeping an eye on the major models, as well as habitually monitoring Gibson's marketing moves. In the late 1960s, guitarists had begun to rediscover Gibson's old Les Paul models, and finally in 1968 Gibson re-introduced the early-style single-cutaway model for which almost everyone seemed to be clamouring. Gretsch responded by bringing back their own discontinued single-cutaway solidbody design, last seen in 1961 in the form of the single-cut Jets and Chet Solid. Gretsch launched the $350 Roc Jet in 1969, and shortly afterwards dropped the remaining twin-cutaway Jet models.

A BIG CHET IS A SUPER CHET

In the Booneville-factory era, Baldwin must surely have decided that they may as well exploit the contract they had with Chet Atkins that ensured his involvement with Gretsch for a number of years. In 1972 a new Gretsch Chet Atkins design hit the market in the shape of two broadly similar models, the Deluxe Chet and the Super Chet.

These big single-cutaway archtops – the bodies were 17 inches wide and two-and-a-half inches deep – resulted from a collaboration between Chet Atkins, Dean Porter and Clyde Edwards. Porter was described by Gretsch as their "master technician" – and as Atkins has already told us, was the man who "got the guitars so they would play" – while Edwards was Gretsch's "master string-instrument designer". A company newsletter of the time said: "The surest way of getting this super guitar was to turn these three men loose and tell them to design the best guitar they could, no holds barred. ... More fussing went into this guitar than you can imagine."

A lot of the fussing must have been spent on the profuse decorative work on the Super Chet, which had flowery inlays sprouting on the fingerboard, the headstock and the tailpiece. It also sported an unusual row of control 'wheels' built into the edge of the pickguard, and was decorated with an attractive inlaid centre stripe around the body sides. Atkins was responsible for this, as he told me. "I had a little acoustic guitar from the 1800s that a lady had given me. It had a lot of inlay on it, and inlay in the centre of the sides, so I had them do that. We were trying to make a really beautiful guitar. Clyde just tried to build the prettiest guitar ever." The Deluxe Chet was a plainer version, with conventional controls and none of the foliage, and did not last long. The Super Chet stayed in the line for about seven years, and was reissued as the Super Gretsch in 1998.

FROM CLIPPER TO FALCON, EARLY SEVENTIES STYLE

The August 1972 pricelist showed 14 electric models in the Booneville-made Gretsch line, of which 13 are archtops: the Clipper was listed at $250; the Anniversary two-pickup at $345; Streamliner at $395 (a lower-price twin-cutaway archtop launched in 1968); Chet Atkins Tennessean $495; Country Club $500 sunburst, $525 natural; Chet Atkins Nashville 6120 $595 (this was the 6120's new official name since about 1967); Van Eps seven-string $675; Chet Atkins Country Gentleman $695; Viking $700 sunburst, $725 natural; Deluxe Chet $750; Super Chet $850; White Falcon $975; and White Falcon Stereo $1,100. The solitary solid was the single-cutaway Roc Jet at $395 in red, orange or black, $425 in brown.

The odd Gretsch Roc II appeared in 1973. It was a single-cutaway solid that had an elliptical control plate with circuitry intended to produce copious quantities of treble and distortion. "High degree of treble booster for 'screaming' rock sounds," said the press release. "No thank you," said most guitarists.

Following on from 1969's Roc Jet, which was partly prompted by a growing sense of nostalgia among players for older-style instruments, Gretsch added the Country Roc to the line in 1974, a Western-appointed solidbody that evoked but hardly matched the Round Up model of the 1950s. In the same year Gretsch re-introduced a single-cutaway deep-body mono White Falcon, a model last made with this kind of body style some 12 years earlier. The 'new' Falcon partnered the contemporary twin-cutaway thinline mono and stereo versions. It was significant as the first reissue or 'retro' Gretsch archtop, and underlined the growing fashion for using old guitars.

Some guitarists were becoming convinced that older instruments were somehow more playable and sounded better than new guitars. Norman's Rare Guitars, established in California during the mid 1970s, was one of the newer dealers specialising in the 'vintage' requirements of rock players. Proprietor Norman Harris was in no doubt why so many guitarists were taking up older instruments – like those he offered for sale. "You simply cannot compare what I have to offer with what the big companies are mass producing today," he boasted in 1976.

> Some guitarists in the 1970s were becoming convinced that older so-called 'vintage' instruments were somehow more playable and sounded better than new guitars.

STEPHEN STILLS AND THE DRESSING ROOM OF GRETSCH

By that same year Stephen Stills, ex-Crosby Stills & Nash, had amassed a collection of some 70 guitars. Touring with his solo band at the time he needed two dressing rooms: one for himself, another for the 17 guitars that accompanied him on the road. Included

NEW GUITARS, OLD GUITARS

▲ 1993 Country Classic II 6122-1962

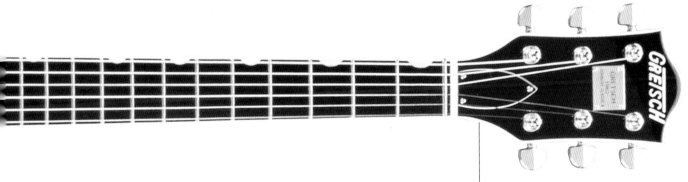

The first guitars from a revived Gretsch came in 1989, among them the Traveling Wilbury (ad, far left), against a background of yet more players picking up older Gretsches. Brian Setzer (above) was heading a rockabilly revival in The Stray Cats with his '59 6120; Billy Duffy in The Cult and Robert Smith of The Cure (left) played single-cut oldies; and John Squire of The Stone Roses (opposite, top) played a 60s Country Gent. New Gretsches echoed the past too, but for legal reasons some were renamed, like this 60s-style Gent (main guitar), now a Country Classic.

were five old Gretsches: two Falcons and three Country Gents. "I don't think they've built anything new that's worth a damn since 1965," he told *Guitar Player*. "It's all mechanised." This quote from Stills neatly popularised the notion that it was somehow only old guitars that were worthy of attention by 'real' players. The first published attempt to sort out the various old Gretsch models and their dates of manufacture had come in Tom Wheeler's *The Guitar Book* a few years earlier.

> "It's not as though they're playing. It's more like a conversation. I mean, it's been four years since they held a conversation like that, and they've a hell of a lot to say to one another."
> *David Crosby on Gretsch-wielding bandmates Steve Stills and Neil Young, 1974*

Other players were discovering the charms of Gretsch. Pete Townshend had used a 6120 given to him by Joe Walsh for the raucous noise sprayed over most of the 1971 *Who's Next* album, as well as 1973's *Quadrophenia*. Despite the fact that he largely avoided the guitar on stage because it "won't stay in tune", Townshend said in 1972: "It's the best guitar I've ever had … and the loudest."

Around that same time, in Crosby Stills Nash & Young, Stephen Stills and bandmate Neil Young had spearheaded the early-1970s Gretsch revival. Young's Falcon-assisted intro to CSNY's summer '70 Top 20 hit 'Ohio' was more than enough to satisfy many Gretsch fans. Sometimes at the band's concerts it was possible to see three Gretsches on the go at once, with Young often wielding a multi-control stereo Falcon that provided a visual as well as aural treat. David Crosby was naturally well positioned to observe many guitar duels between Stills and Young. "It's not as though they're playing," he told an interviewer during the CSNY reunion tour of 1974. "It's more like they're having a conversation. I mean … it's been four years since they last held a conversation like that, and they've a hell of a lot to say to one another."

Meanwhile at Gretsch HQ, they decided to put out two new cheaper guitars in 1975, the Broadkaster solidbody and semi-hollow electrics. As usual, Gretsch was to some extent following Gibson's lead – and on this occasion the path was an unpopular one. Gibson had launched the Marauder, its first solidbody guitar with a Fender-style bolt-on neck, in 1974; likewise, the Broadkaster solid was the first Gretsch with a bolt-on neck, and also displayed strong influences of Stratocaster styling. Neither model raised much interest.

Baldwin had added a Japanese-made solidbody electric to its catalogue around 1972 under the Dorado brandname, separate from Gretsch but significant because it was the company's first involvement with oriental guitar manufacturing. The connection brought dividends four years later when a Japanese supplier was chosen to provide new pickups for several Gretsch models.

Ray Butts's patent for the Filter'Tron pickup reached the end of its official 17-year run in 1976. The previous year he'd received a letter from Gretsch advising that royalty payments would end. Butts recalled: "I had made a handshake agreement on my humbucking pickup with Mr Gretsch. He told me they'd done business that way with K Zildjian in Turkey, the cymbal manufacturers, for over 50 years, and also with Cuesnon band instruments of France. So we had no written agreement, which was fine at the time.

"When the company was sold," Butts continued, "Baldwin just sort of forgot about everything. With that letter in '75 they sent me a little money, and said they felt the agreement no longer applied." In the letter, Gretsch also asked Butts if he might like to devise a new pickup for possible use on the Roc Jet and Broadkaster models, as well as on the "new Chet Atkins Hi-Roller model guitar". When Butts understandably declined, Gretsch turned to a Japanese supplier, and soon began fitting cheap-quality 'humbuckers' – which performed suspiciously like single-coils – to the existing Roc Jet and Broadkaster models. (Butts did no more business with Gretsch, the company for whom he had done so much. He died in April 2003.)

CHET ROLLS THE DICE FOR A SUPER AXE

As for the 'Atkins Hi-Roller', this was the original name given to a design that evolved into the new Super Axe and Atkins Axe guitars of 1977. Gretsch was still hazy about a name late in 1976: an ad then mentioned an upcoming instrument to be called the 'Atkins Yakety Axe'. The distinctive look of these big new guitars with their sweeping, pointed cutaway and 16-inch-wide solid bodies was the subject of a patent for ornamental design issued to Gretsch designer Clyde Edwards. Also involved in the project were Chet Atkins and Gretsch general manager Duke Kramer.

"Chet wanted to call it the Hi-Roller guitar," Kramer recalled, "and he wanted to put on dice as position markers. We made a few with the dice – we even had it down as the Hi-Roller on a pricelist – but the Baldwin people thought the name and the dice gave the guitar a bad connotation of gambling, and they didn't want that. So we left the markers plain, and we called it the Super Axe. Chet wanted more sustain, so he put on a compressor, and he wanted a phaser on it, which the Baldwin engineers came up with." Brian Setzer would later take up the idea of a Gretsch guitar with dice decorations.

When the two models were launched, the effects-laden version was called the Super Axe and the less expensive no-gadgets option the Atkins Axe – despite the fact that it was Chet who originated the idea for the built-in electronic effects. Nonetheless, he appeared in Gretsch's ads at the time pushing the Super Axe, which was clearly the version he liked. Some of this confusion was probably caused by Gretsch seeking an endorsement deal with country guitarist Roy Clark. Kramer said that the company decided not to put Chet Atkins's name on the new guitars. "We were going to pay Chet a royalty because he helped design them, but we weren't going to have his name on them. I took one out to Roy Clark, and he fell in love with it. He wanted to play it, and I said OK … we might make it the Roy Clark model. He said that'd be great. I got back and told Chet, and he didn't like that at all, so we never did it – although Roy did use and play the guitar, and we did some advertising with him." The Atkins Axe would be reissued as the Axe in 1996.

Gretsch added a couple more solidbody electrics to the line in 1977, the TK-300 and the Committee. The TK-300 was another cheap solid with bolt-on neck, this time with a strange asymmetric body. The Committee followed a trend of the time for through-neck construction, where the neck runs the complete length of the guitar with added 'wings' to complete the body shape. Both were uninspiring guitars by any standards, almost totally lacking in the character that had once been at the heart of Gretsch design.

A pricelist from April 1977 summed up the Gretsch line of 18 electrics. There were 11 archtops: the Broadkaster at $495 in sunburst or natural ($550 with vibrato), $525 red; Anniversary two-pickup $625; Chet Atkins Tennessean $695; Country Club $725 Antique Maple, $750 natural; Chet Atkins Nashville 6120 $795; Van Eps seven-string $795; Chet

SEE POLLY PLAY GRETSCH

▼ 1995 Sparkle Jet 6129T

1960 6120 Nashville Reissue

GRETSCH

The Nashville is often considered to be the most popular Gretsch electric guitar. Introduced in 1954, the Nashville has become standard issue for generations of country, rockabilly, and rock'n'roll players. This reintroduced 1960 model Nashville optimizes the design, playability, and sound of the first generation 6120.

1993 Nashville Brian Setzer 6120SSUGR ▶

P.J. Harvey (right) often opted for a late-70s Broadkaster on stage, but Brian Setzer (left) stuck to his rockabilly-cred 6120 — even when he shifted to a big-band phase. Gretsch could not have missed Setzer's popularity and the fact that he was one of the most visible of Gretsch players, and in 1993 a 'signature' Setzer model appeared (right, and Japanese ad, left). Meanwhile, Gretsch was busy giving a new spin to some old ideas, such as this 'blue pearl'-finished Jet (main guitar). And while the general theme if not the detail was to recreate the best of the past, Gretsch tried a little harder in 1992 with the 6120-1960 (above).

Atkins Country Gentleman $895; White Falcon single-cutaway $1,050; Super Chet $1,150 hardtail, $1,200 vibrato; White Falcon twin-cutaway mono $1,175; and White Falcon twin-cutaway stereo $1,295. There were seven solids: the TK-300 at $295; Broadkaster $450; Committee $475; Roc Jet $595 black or red, $600 Walnut; Country Roc $695; Atkins Axe $750; and Super Axe $895.

The last new Gretsch guitars to appear under Baldwin ownership were the Beast solids, launched in 1979. These came in different styles, some with a single-cutaway body something like a scaled-down Super Axe, as well as a couple of twin-cutaway versions. Gretsch seemed to want to be all things to all guitarists with the Beasts, absorbing design elements from Gibson and Fender as well as contemporary Japanese makers.

"All the sound you can ask for," boasted a Beastly promotional leaflet. "New pickups, new electronics, completely new designs make it all happen." They ranged in price from $299.50 for a one-pickup bolt-on-neck model to $695 for a two-pickup through-neck guitar. The Beasts seemed functional rather than inspirational, and although few people realised at the time – "this is only the beginning of what you can expect from the Beast family" said that optimistic ad – they would be the last gasp from Gretsch in the 1970s, marking the end of an era with a depressingly low note.

BALDWIN DECIDE TO CALL IT A DAY

If Baldwin's performance in handling their fresh acquisition was measured by the aptitude and success of the new Gretsch models they launched in the 1970s, then their score would be low. They fared little better in the business affairs surrounding Gretsch. Although sales had picked up a little for Gretsch in the early 1970s, still Baldwin were not seeing a profit from the business, despite the various cost-cutting exercises they had made. In early 1973 there had been a bad fire at the factory, adding to the general gloom, and Baldwin decided to contract the manufacture of Gretsch products to long-standing factory manager Bill Hagner.

He formed the Hagner Musical Instrument Corp for the purpose, still operating from the Booneville site. "They didn't want to be bothered with it any more," remembered Hagner, "and assuming that I knew what I was doing they decided to take a chance and do it that way." Another fire at the end of 1973 had not helped these new plans.

At the very start of 1976, Hagner opened a revitalised factory at Booneville – reported at the time as a "re-opening" with the building described as "a spanking new plant affirming Gretsch plans to grow". It seems likely from this that there was little production during 1974 and 1975. The Hagner manufacturing deal ceased at the end of 1978, when control passed back fully to Baldwin. In early 1979 Baldwin bought the Kustom amplifier company and by the end of the year had merged Gretsch with Kustom, moving the sales and administration office for the new combined operation to Chanute, Kansas.

Given the turmoil of the 1970s, Baldwin finally decided that they'd had enough and would stop production of Gretsch guitars. This probably happened some time during 1980, and it seems that very little new product was manufactured beyond the start of 1981 (just short of Gretsch's 100th anniversary, due in 1983). Gretsch drums continued to be made at Booneville until '81, when the business was transferred to a Baldwin factory in De Queen, Arkansas, about 80 miles south of Booneville, and later to Texarkana,

Arkansas, even further south. A man called Charlie Roy was running the Gretsch/Kustom operation, and in early 1982 he bought it from Baldwin, moving his offices then to Gallatin, Tennessee, just outside Nashville. By now Chet Atkins's endorsement deal had come to a natural end, and he soon transferred allegiance to Gibson, who began making a Chet Atkins Country Gentleman model from 1986 and a Chet Atkins Tennessean four years later. Gretsch has never used any Atkins-related names since. A Gibson spokesman said in 2004: "The names have been in use by Gibson for more than five years – a condition for trademark status – so Gibson would undoubtedly claim the names and take action to stop Gretsch or anyone else from using them."

Charlie Roy probably continued to sell his existing Gretsch guitar stock as late as 1983. The last known Kustom/Gretsch pricelist is dated January '83 and shows only Committee and Beast models, presumably leftovers. Baldwin again took control of the Gretsch company soon after this, when the deal with Roy ceased. Around that time some Country Gents were renamed with a label declaring them as 'Southern Belle' models and dating them from around the middle months of 1983. There was a last-ditch plan to revive Gretsch guitar production at a Baldwin piano-action factory in Ciudad Juarez, Mexico, but probably only a small trial batch was assembled, and the idea was then dropped.

Dick Harrison, who had become chief executive officer at Baldwin in 1972, told me that his company – by the late 1970s officially known as Baldwin United – was undergoing dramatic changes. "By the early 1980s it had become predominantly a financial services company, and the music [division] was always doing well but was a very small part of the total." Baldwin's musical strength was in its piano and organ business, he emphasised, and recalled that, despite all the efforts, they never did well with Gretsch guitars, amplifiers or drums. "Baldwin United went bankrupt in September 1983. Out of that, the music company was purchased by myself and another gentleman. We completed the deal by June of 1984." The new Baldwin Piano & Organ Co then proceeded to sell Kustom, after which they turned their attention to Gretsch.

This is the point at which yet another Fred Gretsch came into the picture. It wasn't Fred Gretsch Jr – he had died at age 75 in 1980 – but one of his nephews, whom we shall call Fred Gretsch III. Fred's father was Bill Gretsch, who had run the company from 1942 until his premature death six years later.

It's worth remembering that in the 1980s there was little interest in Gretsch guitars in the US much beyond collectors on a quest to complete their set of Beatle-related axes. There was also Wendy Melvoin of Prince's band, seen in the 'Kiss' video playing a 6120, or Brian Setzer of The Stray Cats heading up a rockabilly revival – of which more later. Dealers such as New Jersey-based Guitar Trader would sell the occasional White Falcon or early 6120 for over $1,000, but other Gretsches went for a great deal less.

In Britain, a number of guitarists were attracted by these relatively affordable 'old' guitars that looked the part and played OK. It seemed almost de rigueur for Scottish

> **British guitarists flocked to Gretsches in the 1980s, including Edwyn Collins of Orange Juice with a Black Hawk, The Cult's Billy Duffy with a White Falcon, Robert Smith of The Cure with a Tennessean, and John Squire of The Stone Roses with a Country Gent.**

SIGN RIGHT HERE PLEASE

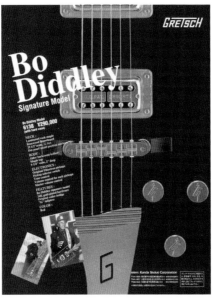

Still the new interpretations of oldies poured out of Gretsch's Japanese factory, not least the colourful Jets that included a gold Sparkle version (main guitar). Some stranger items began to pop up too, and among the oddest were two new double-neck models, a departure for Gretsch in terms of production models. Double-necks are certainly specialist instruments, designed to give you an instant switch on stage, usually between a six-string and a 12-string. Just such a choice was offered on 1997's new 6120 double-necker (right), and a year later on a Duo Jet. Gretsch joined Fender, Gibson and the rest in the 1990s by issuing a slew of signature models, including an 'aged finish' White Falcon named for longtime Gretsch devotee Stephen Stills (ad, far left). There was also room in the expanding Gretsch line for official issue of the remarkable rectangular-body Bo Diddley guitar, aptly captured in the company's almost identically shaped advertisement (left).

▲ **1998 Sparkle Jet 6129T**

▲ 1997 Nashville 6120-6/12 double-neck

Duane Eddy was finally honoured with a 'signature' model in 1997. As expected, it was based on his famous 6120, but was offered in 'blackburst' (ad, far right) as well as orange. A few years later the model was dropped when Duane switched allegiance to Gibson. Keith Scott of the Bryan Adams band came up with a good looking gold-top 6120 for his signature Gretsch (ad, right), first put on sale in 1999. Meanwhile, new players continued to discover Gretsch, like Mudhoney's Mark Arm (above).

bands of the time to include a Gretsch – for instance Edwyn Collins of Orange Juice with an unusual Black Hawk, a shortlived late-'60s double-cut model. Further south, there was The Cure's Robert Smith playing a red 60s Tennessean on-stage, Billy Duffy of The Cult, rarely far from his 70s Falcon, John Squire of The Stone Roses using a 60s Gent around the time of the band's acclaimed first album, and even Martin Gore of the synth-laden Depeche Mode bravely strumming an Anniversary. But as far as the fate of brand new Gretsch guitars was concerned, if it hadn't been for our new Fred, then the book you hold may well have finished right here.

AND THEN THERE WAS A NEW FRED GRETSCH

Fred III had Gretsch in his blood, for sure. He'd originally worked at the Gretsch company from 1965 to 1971, starting in product engineering and working on the factory expansion in 1966. "I'd been going to the Brooklyn factory since about 1951 when Fred Sr, my grandfather, took me there as quite a young fellow," he told me. "I probably started going there when I was five years old. He gave me quite a good interest in the business."

Fred III said that when his uncle, Fred Jr, had sold out to the Baldwin company in 1967, he had felt disappointed. Why was that? "Because I was working in the business, and it was my long-term ambition to own it myself one day. But that was going to take another 17 years to achieve."

When he left Gretsch in 1971, Fred III began his own musical-instrument importing and wholesaling business, acquiring the Synsonics brand in 1980 from Mattel and enjoying some success with acoustic and electronic percussion as well as electric guitars. He stayed in touch with Dick Harrison of Baldwin and "kept an eye" on the bankruptcy of the Baldwin parent company. Duke Kramer was brought in to run the Gretsch business again, and it became clear to the two men that Baldwin was ready to sell. "Negotiations began and were ultimately successful in November of 1984, and I bought the business in January of '85," Fred III told me. "The plan was to continue drum making in Arkansas for a year, then to move it to our location in South Carolina, and subsequently to get the guitar business going again."

Kramer told me that they decided to introduce updated versions of the classic Gretsch models of the past, and he drew up specifications for the proposed new models. Then they had to find someone to manufacture the new guitars. Kramer visited quite a few American makers, including Heritage (ex-Gibson workers located in the old Gibson factory in Kalamazoo, Michigan), Guild, and Gibson itself, but no deal was reached for electric models. "So then our only option was to go offshore," explained Kramer, using the US term for anything made outside the country. "I went to Japan and selected Terada. They were used to making hollowbody guitars, whereas the rest were used to making mainly solidbody guitars."

In 1989 Gretsch offered an unusual forerunner to the forthcoming new line with a series of Korean-made electrics intended to capitalise on the popularity of the Traveling Wilburys, a fictional family supergroup consisting of George Harrison ('Nelson Wilbury'), Jeff Lynne ('Otis'), Bob Dylan ('Lucky'), Tom Petty ('Charlie T Jr') and Roy Orbison ('Lefty'). These cheap and somewhat primitive guitars were loosely based on the group's old Danelectro instruments, and various models were issued, all boldly finished in what Gretsch called "original graphics" with an appropriate travel theme.

Fred Gretsch Enterprises Ltd delivered its first proper Gretsch guitars to dealers by the second half of 1989. With the company no longer able to use the names of Chet Atkins and associated models following the guitarist's earlier defection to Gibson, some of the model names were necessarily modified, while others remained familiar.

The September 1989 pricelist showed nine electric models. There were five archtops: the Tennessee Rose (the post-Chet politically-correct name for a Tennessean) at $1,495; the Nashville (a plain 6120) at $1,750; Nashville Western (6120 with G-brand etc) at $1,875; Country Classic single cutaway (a Country Gentleman single-cut) at $1,975; and the Country Classic twin cutaway (double-cut Gent) at $1,975. There were four solids: the Duo Jet at $1,300; Silver Jet at $1,400; Jet Firebird $1,400; and Round Up $1,550. By 1990 a pair of White Falcon models had been added, single or twin-cutaway, for nearly $3,000 each, and, as we shall see, further reissues followed. The 6120 and White Falcon in particular have appeared in an array of different versions.

> **Brian Setzer and The Stray Cats had personified the early 80s rockabilly revival, but it took Gretsch until 1993 to officially mark his importance by issuing a Brian Setzer model. "I'm their first guitar endorsee since Chet Atkins," said a proud Setzer.**

Brian Setzer and The Stray Cats had personified the rockabilly revival of the early 1980s. Originally, rockabilly was probably the result of country guitarists trying to play rock'n'roll ('rock'n'roll' plus 'hillbilly' makes … 'rockabilly'). Some said that the new '80s popularity was the result of a thirst for music that shared the raw power of punk – but that it was still a 1950s throwback. Setzer, however, has always been more than a mere re-enactor. True, he often displays the trappings of a rockabilly: the hair, the clothes, the 6120, the Bassman amps. But more than all that, Setzer is a fine, versatile guitarist. From the start, the revived Gretsch company had their eye on him as the most visible 1980s user of their instruments – not least that luscious White Falcon he used for the video of 1982's 'Stray Cat Strut' (a number 3 hit in the US and number 11 in Britain). But it took Gretsch until '93 to officially recognise his importance by issuing a Brian Setzer model – by which time he was about to move to big-band swing. "I'm their first guitar endorsee since Chet Atkins," said a proud Setzer.

The new-for-'93 Nashville Brian Setzer model was based on his prime live guitar of the time, a '59 6120 (though, as we shall see, the detail would be significantly improved later). For now, there was a thinner neck and tapered heel, Gibson-style bridge, Sperzel locking tuners, alnico-magnet Filter'Trons, optional dice-pattern square knobs, and a choice of finishes (regular polyurethane $2,900, 'vintage correct' lacquer $3,350).

SIGNING UP FOR THAT PERSONAL SOUND

More signature guitars followed. A Malcolm Young model appeared in 1996 based on the AC/DC rhythm guitarist's much-modified early-60s double-cut Jet Fire Bird, offered in authentic single as well as twin-pickup versions ($1,595-$1,895). A $3,700 Keith Scott Nashville – effectively a gold-top single-coil 6120 – was launched in 1999; before that, Scott had often used a White Falcon on-stage and in the studio with his boss Bryan Adams. A trio of interesting signatures came along in 2000: green and red single-cut longer-scale Jets for ex-Cars man Elliot Easton ($2,750-$3,050); the inevitable rectangular

FROM HOT ROD TO BARITONE

▲ 2001 Nashville Western 6120W-1957

▲ 2003 Nashville Brian Setzer Hot Rod 6120SH

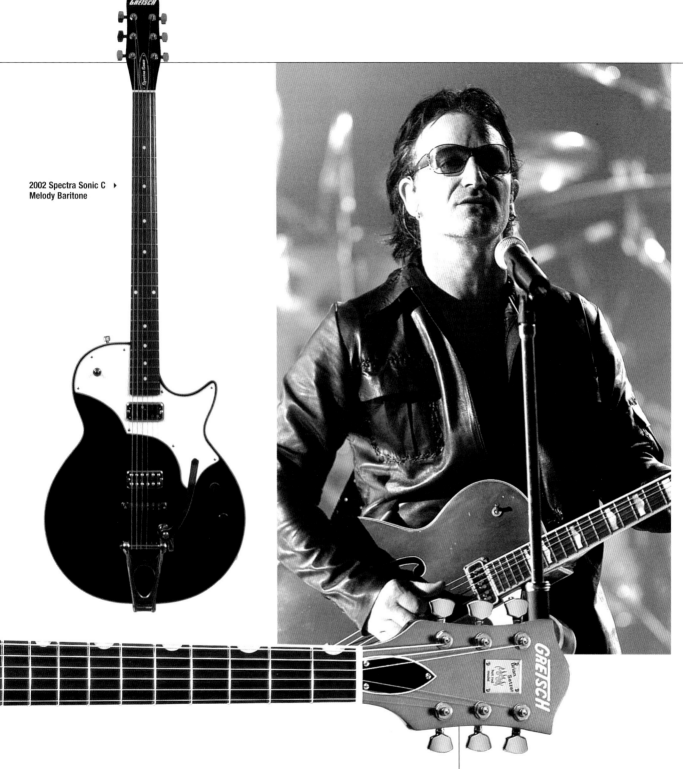

2002 Spectra Sonic C ▸
Melody Baritone

Signature models, re-creations of the past, brand new models, famous players: all were part of the Gretsch landscape as the company entered the 21st century. Brian Setzer had a new signature model to sit alongside the existing one. The Hot Rod (main guitar) was a kind of simplified 6120, with just a single volume knob and pickup selector, and came in car-crazy colours. New for 2001 was the Nashville Western 1957 (opposite, top), nothing less than an Eddie Cochran 6120, complete with his favoured P-90 pickup at the neck. The Spectra Sonic was a development of T.V. Jones's Danelectro-flavoured guitar, seen here (above) in its intriguing baritone format, effectively a regular guitar tuned down a couple of tones and with a longer scale length, adding up to a dark brown voice. Meanwhile the voice of U2 was seen fronting his band with a Gretsch, here (above) a Country Club.

Bo Diddley model ($2,500); and an 'aged finish' single-cut White Falcon named for Stephen Stills ($4,500) and complete with a special inlaid signature on the upper fingerboard. Then in 2005 Gretsch offered a further rockabilly treat, the Reverend Horton Heat signature G-brand 6120, plus a second Diddley guitar, the remarkably streamlined Jupiter Thunderbird.

ONCE MORE WITH FEELING FOR CHET AND EDDIE AND DUANE

Beyond the signature guitars already mentioned, Gretsch has offered models honouring all three of their most famous 1950s players, the guitarists upon whom much of the Gretsch legend is built. The first of these came along in 1997 when, at last, Gretsch acknowledged the king of twang with a $3,700 Duane Eddy model, based on his original single-coil 6120 – though by the end of 2003 it was gone from the catalogue. The reason? Duane had defected to Gibson. Fred III told me: "Duane has good friends at Gibson too, and they live almost next door. We're best of friends, but sometimes the neighbours win out. That year we were honoured at a Grammy event in Atlanta and Duane did our introduction – and this was after we knew he was doing custom things with Gibson. So the relationship is strong. Sometimes an individual player will marry a brand for life, and sometimes they won't. For example, our relationship with [Aerosmith's] Joe Perry is wonderful, but he's a contract guy with Gibson – but he plays whatever he damn well pleases."

> The new 'Nashville Classic' is a re-creation of Chet's 1959 Country Gent. Pity it can't be called a Chet Atkins Country Gentleman, because that's exactly what it is.

The second model saluting Gretsch's key 1950s players was 2001's Nashville Western 57 ($3,000), in all but name an Eddie Cochran 6120. It has the great man's favoured P-90 in the neck position and a see-through pickguard – Eddie allegedly scraped the gold backing from his to achieve transparency. But for some reason doubtless connected with lawyers the Nashville Western does not have the Cochran name attached. However, a Cochran model is certainly what it is.

And finally in the trio of great 50s players' Gretsches comes the Nashville Classic, first issued in 2003 at $3,475, a re-creation of Chet Atkins's 1959 single-cut Country Gentleman, complete with Chet's long-fixed-arm Bigsby. Paul Yandell, the Nashville guitarist who worked regularly with Atkins from 1975, helped bring the guitar into production. "I thought it would be nice to have that old Gent redone," Yandell told me. "Gretsch had a version of that model, but it wasn't like the old ones. Chet had played his for about 30 years and cut most of his records with it, and he'd made some changes to it that improved it considerably. It's down at the Hall Of Fame here in Nashville."

What were the mods Chet had made? "He'd asked Gretsch to make it with a wider neck because he liked that. Then he changed the wiring on it. He eliminated the tone switch up the top and made one of the controls down the bottom a tone. The other control down there he kept as volume on the back pickup. He figured that you really don't need a volume on the front pickup if you've got a master volume, because when you've got both pickups on, you can always turn down the back one. Also, he rewound the back pickup to 8k instead of 4k to get more output for recording. Other than that, it was a stock Gent. He said it sustained real good, and that was one reason he liked it. It was a wonderful guitar." TV Jones designed and made the pickups: a flat-blade Super'Tron at the neck, and a darker-toned open-cover Filter'Tron at the neck. Recently, this Nashville Classic has been made even more faithful to the original.

"They made new moulds for it," Yandell told me in 2004, "and the shape and everything is now identical to the old ones. I think the Nashville Classic is better than the original, because I had one back then." Pity it can't be called a Chet Atkins Country Gentleman because, again, that's exactly what it is.

From the mid 1990s Gretsch came up with a few more new models, including in 1996 the first of a series of down-sized versions of its regular models, the $2,000 Nashville Junior, and a 12-string Country Classic. A year later saw the first double-neck, the $5,000 Nashville 6/12, followed in 1998 by the $4,500 Duo Jet 6/12. Reissues came along too. In 1993 there was a brief modern outing for the revered White Penguin, which reappeared in 2003 at $5,225.

Also in 1993 the Anniversary was reissued in single-pickup ($1,500) or twin-pickup ($1,700) versions, and the same year saw a more successful attempt at recreating an original 6120 with the $2,075 6120-60. The Axe (1996, $2,100) and Super Gretsch (1998, $3,000) revisited the 1970s solidbody Atkins Axe and hollowbody Super Chet models, and a single-cut '55-style Country Club was launched in 1996 at $7,500. (There's been no sign yet of a reissue for the multi-control stereo models; perhaps Gretsch is waiting for a Neil Young signature Falcon?)

TOP DOLLAR AT THE CUSTOM SHOP

That '55-style Country Club came at such a high price because it was among the first of a new series of Custom USA models, made not in the regular Japanese factory but at home in the States, at Gretsch plants in Ridgeland, South Carolina, and in Arkansas. (A regular Japanese-made Country Club would appear in 2001, at $3,700.) First shown at a trade show in 1995, the Custom Shop Country Club was accompanied by two more ultimate '55-style US-made reissues: an $8,500 White Falcon and a $7,000 Nashville Custom (6120).

"Joe Walsh was one of the visitors at our booth," Fred III told me, "and he fell in love with the 6120-1955 we had there and wanted to buy it. We told him we don't sell our first prototypes, but if we did we would make it available to him. He called several times after that to twist arms and, to make a long story short, we arranged for him to purchase that guitar though a favourite dealer."

But this brave attempt at American manufacture didn't last long: production stopped in 1998 and the models were gone from the pricelist by 2000. Only recently has the experiment been revived, starting in 2004 at Fender's Custom Shop.

Gretsch's Korean-made Electromatic-brand guitars with Gretsch-like features first appeared as a line exclusively for sale by the US Guitar Center chain of stores in the late 1990s – including the gloriously named Mini Diddley model, a smaller rectangle for diminutive Bo fans. Similar lines with Synchromatic and Historic brands, for sale by other dealers through distributor Midco, came along in 2000. More recently, the Historic brand has been dropped and the Synchromatics gradually phased out, leaving the Korean and Chinese-made Electromatics as the less expensive line – and now bearing a proper Gretsch logo on the headstock with a little 'Electromatic' underneath.

YOURS ELECTROMATICLY

▲ 2003 White Penguin

▲ 2003 Nashville Classic 6122-1959

2004 ▶
Electromatic
Junior Jet II

Despite the great man's death in 2001, Chet Atkins's influence on Gretsch guitars and Gretsch players shows no sign of waning. A suitable tribute came two years later with the Nashville Classic (main guitar), an accurate re-creation of Chet's long-serving 1959 Country Gentleman. Also in 2003 the White Penguin (left, top) was back in the fold. Gretsch used a number of brands for its budget models, but recently settled on Electromatic (Junior Jet, above). Elsewhere the company stressed its heritage with a 120th Anniversary model (ad right), while Fountains Of Wayne (above) mixed old and new Gretsches for a fresh sound.

The first Gretsch that Tom 'TV' Jones saw up close was one of Brian Setzer's 6120s, a guitar that Setzer was given by Steve Miller and used in the late 1980s and early '90s. Jones was working at a guitar shop in Long Beach, California, and in came the guitar with tech Rich Modica. In August '93 Jones was asked to do a fret job on the same instrument, and has worked on Setzer's guitars ever since, often together with Modica. It was Modica who hooked up Jones with Gretsch.

"Rich asked me to develop a pickup for the new Setzer Hot Rod guitar that Brian was working on with Gretsch," Jones told me. "It needed to be a pickup that sounded more like the original Filter'Trons than the ones they were using. So then he introduced me to Mr Gretsch."

FILTER'TRON MAGIC, TAKE TWO

Gretsch sent Jones to study the production process in the Tokiwa factory in Japan that manufactures most of the company's pickups. Jones then set to work and turned up some old magnet material and authentic Fillister cylinder-head pole screws (rather than the dome-head types then being used). "The key to the Filter'Tron had to do with the materials and the way the wire was wound," Jones said, "the tension, and how fine or coarse the magnet wire is layered on the bobbin as you wind it, like a thread on a screw. Also, I widened the pole spacing on the TV Jones bridge pickups from November 1999 to get a more independent string sound and output."

Jones made some samples, organised a blind test with other pickups – and Setzer loved the one by TV Jones. "In November '98 Mr Gretsch came by my shop and asked me if I'd like to work as a consultant and help to design guitars with recording artists and also help him generally with guitar stuff. I said yes! It's been a great time."

Jones now designs and makes custom Gretsch pickups for selected models. (Seymour Duncan supplies the single-coil DynaSonics for the current US Custom Shop 6120; all other pickups are made for Gretsch by Tokiwa in Japan.) The TV Jones business has boomed, moving in 2001 from Whittier, California (near Los Angeles) to new, expanded premises in Washington State, where at the time of writing the firm employs seven people.

The new Setzer Hot Rod guitar appeared in 1999 at $2,750, alongside the existing signature model. It's still a 6120 at heart, but visually is somewhat startling. Not only does it come in a range of vibrant car-crazy colours – including Candy Apple Red, Lime Gold, Tangerine, and Purple – but has a simple two-control layout, just a volume knob and a pickup selector, as well as the option of those Jones Filter'Trons. And recently the design has been significantly improved thanks to something you'd never normally notice.

Setzer's famous '59 6120 – which he'd bought in the 1970s for $100 – was made during a relatively brief period when the body featured a particular kind of internal bracing. Under the top are two parallel 'tone bars', or braces, that run the length of the body and to which the pickups are screwed. From about '58 to '61, two twin-leg 'trestles' were added to each bar, with one leg near the bridge and one near the neck, effectively connecting the guitar's top to its back at four points.

Gretsch incorporated these 'trestles' into the new Hot Rods – and now the Nashville Setzer too – and the result, they claim, is an extremely solid feeling guitar, with noticeably more sustain, less feedback, and a 'looser' acoustic quality – because the top and the back are now vibrating more sympathetically with one another. The new Hot Rods have a number of other improvements, including thinner bodies with three-ply tops and backs rather than the five-ply of regular 1990s Gretsches. Meanwhile, in 1999 Gretsch bought the Bigsby Accessories company, owned since the mid 1960s by ex-Gibson boss Ted McCarty. This seemed like a natural move: the basic wang-bar had first become associated with Gretsches when Chet Atkins insisted that it be included on the 6120, and since then many of us have found a bit of gentle arm to be an important part of the Gretsch sound.

Following the success of the new TV Jones Filter'Tron, Fred III had Jones begin work on a new Tokiwa-produced HiLo'Tron, the single-coil pickup that Gretsch had first used back in the late 1950s. The first public appearance of this remodelled pickup came in 2002 with a revised Tennessee Rose variant, the $2,400 1962HT model that recalled George Harrison's Beatle-period Tennessean. (Jones also offers a HiLo'Tron among his TV Jones line of custom replacement pickups.)

As a guitar maker, Jones had built a few of his Danelectro-flavoured Spectra Sonic models for players like John Fogerty, but decided to build a baritone version – that's one tuned down a couple of tones – for Rich Modica, who in turn introduced Brian Setzer to the instrument. Setzer, who by now had gone beyond rockabilly and into swing, liked to play in keys that suited the brass players in his big-band. A sax-playing friend told Jones that C tuning for guitar would work well for this.

Setzer loved the Jones bari and used it on his 2000 tour. Fred III saw Setzer play that guitar during a show in Atlanta and wondered if it could become a Gretsch model. He and Jones and Modica devised a baritone and a bass to add to Jones's guitar design, resulting in the new US-made Gretsch Spectra Sonic line launched in 2002. At the time of writing Gretsch is working on revised versions that will be made in Japan.

Also new for 2002 were the New Jet models with their flame tops and bigger than usual headstocks, the result of a request from a US retail chain who wanted a guitar with a Gretsch look and a Les Paul tone. They were gone from the pricelist by 2004.

The Hot Rod joined Brian Setzer's signature model and comes in vibrant car-crazy colours including Candy Apple Red, Lime Gold, Tangerine, and Purple. It also boasts a very simple control layout: just a volume knob and a pickup switch.

FENDER LOVES GRETSCH, TRUE

Gretsch made moves towards an alliance with Fender during 2002, officially registered with a press statement in August headed "Fender & Gretsch join forces". The two companies said they were proud to announce an agreement where, effective January 1st 2003, Fender Musical Instruments Corporation was granted the exclusive rights to "develop, produce, market and distribute" Gretsch guitars worldwide. Which to most people must have sounded like a buy-out. Not so, Fred III told me. "There were some key markets where we were challenged to provide excellent distribution, for example Europe and the UK. We talked to our friends, and Bill Schultz at Fender was one of them. We talked about them taking distribution for Gretsch in Europe and the UK – and Bill said

AND SO TO THE SEVENTH DECADE

▼ 2004 White Falcon 6136CST

In the sixth decade of electric guitar making, the Gretsch story is far from over – yet our version must end here. And with the guitars on these two pages it has come full circle, for these are new made-in-America custom shop versions of the two electrics that began the saga back in 1955. The White Falcon (main guitar) and Chet Atkins 6120 (right, and correct 'cowboy' case) established the tone for the flamboyance and player-cred that has been right at the heart of Gretschness ever since. As we've seen, there have been some deviations. Billy Gibbons of ZZ Top (right) models for us one of the most bizarre, a weird-shape Bo Diddley thing that Gretsch is planning to issue in 2005 as the Jupiter Thunderbird. But with the continuing support of players (like Brian Setzer: ad, left) Gretsch looks set for many more decades of unique, sleek, whacky and unquestionably cool guitars.

2004 Nashville Western 6120WCST ▶

they'd like to do it worldwide. "Bill started his career in the music business working for Gretsch in about 1960, in the band-instruments section. He worked quite successfully there, and then was recruited to Yamaha and CBS, moved to Fender, and now heads that company. So we have a warm relationship with Bill that goes way back. Plus we had worked with Fender's team before when we did a limited run of Broadcaster guitars, which we allowed them to do as we owned the name," explained Fred. "We looked at Fender as number one in the world, with great resources. Their proposal was: let us take over the distribution and manufacturing worldwide and we'll really build this business together. And that's what happened. We still own and control the brand, and they do the marketing, manufacturing and distribution."

THERE'S ONLY ONE GRETSCH

Fender have never had much acceptance for their own hollowbody electrics. They'd clearly been thinking about Gretsch in the years before the hook-up, whether it was simply the look of those DynaSonic-style pickups on their De Armond brand, a second-tier line they introduced a few years after buying Guild in 1995, or the distinctly Gretsch-flavoured Fender D'Aquisto Classic Rocker model of 2000.

> "We looked at Fender as number one in the world, with great resources," said Fred Gretsch III. Fender was granted the exclusive rights to "develop, produce, market and distribute" Gretsch guitars worldwide, effective January 1st 2003.

"But there's only one Gretsch," said Mike Lewis, Fender's newly appointed marketing manager for Gretsch. "If you do anything that just sort of looks like Gretsch, it's kind of a joke. It's either the real thing or it's stupid."

Lewis told me he thinks of the Gretsch fan in a similar way to the Harley Davidson fan. "It's part of their lifestyle. The Harley guy knows that there's other brands out there that may be more efficient, or more high performance, or better on gas mileage, or lower priced. But he doesn't care. He wants that Harley. Same thing with the Gretsch guy. He wants that Gretsch."

According to Fender, since the end of 2002 virtually every specification of every model has been changed. The new alliance has also introduced a number of new models, and revamped the Brian Setzer line. To help them decide what to change in the specs, Fender went out and bought some vintage Gretsch guitars – just as they had when they worked on the first proper Fender reissues over 20 years ago. George Blanda in Fender R&D already owned a '55 Country Club, which also served for single-cut Falcon specs. But they had to buy a '61 6120, a '64 Anniversary, and a '59 6121 Solid Body, and borrowed a '55 White Falcon and a '55 6120 from Gretsch nut Randy Bachman for the Custom Shop models. "Our guys there completely reverse-engineered them," said Mike Lewis. He means they copied them, very accurately.

As a result, the new Fender-era Gretsches – the regular Japanese-made ones as well as the high-end US Custom Shop instruments begun in 2004 – now have accurate body and headstock shapes and dead-on neck profiles. The guitars have authentically thinner body tops and backs. The pickups are closer to the old specs. Grover machines are used: Sta-Tites and Imperials on vintage models; Rotomatics on modern stuff. The horseshoes are in the right place. Fender insists that they've got it all right. (And one instant way to tell if you have a Fender-period Gretsch is to check the guitar's serial number: at the time of writing almost all of the regular Fender-era instruments have on them an eight-digit serial number preceded by the letters JT, which stands for Japan as country of origin and Terada as factory.)

The summer 2004 pricelist showed 17 electric model names, including a good selection of lefties. There were seven archtops, many offered in a variety of options: Anniversary $2,125-$2,875; Nashville (6120) $2,475-$4,500 (Brian Setzer $3,800-$4,300; Keith Scott $3,975; Double Neck $5,325; US Custom Shop version $8,000); Country Classic (Country Gentleman) $2,500-$3,875; Tennessee Rose (Tennessean) $2,575-$2,675; Setzer Hot Rod $3,075; Country Club $3,375-$3,575; and White Falcon $3,975-$4,125 (Stephen Stills $4,775; US Custom Shop Falcon $10,000).

There were ten solids on that pricelist, also with some offered in a variety of options: Malcolm Young $1,925-$2,225; Duo Jet $2,225-$3,125 (Double Neck $4,800); Jet Firebird $2,325-$2,375; Silver Jet $2,475-$3,025; Sparkle Jet $2,625; Roundup $2,875; Bo Diddley $2,775; Elliot Easton $3,025; Spectra Sonic $3,325-$3,925; White Penguin $3,975.

Most modern Gretsches are still manufactured in Japan by Terada, but with Fender's expertise in offshore production they had some good allies to call upon. The Dyna Gakki factory, which makes a lot of the Fender Japan guitars, seems to have taken a distinct Beatle leaning. As well as the 6120DC, a '62-style with mutes, Dyna makes two new-for-2004 models: the 6122SP, a Beatle/Ed Sullivan-period Gent that has the crucial 'flip-up' mute switches with red felt pads, and the 6128TSP, a Duo Jet based on that first Gretsch of George Harrison's. The Beatle connection is always going to be important to many Gretsch fans.

> "The Harley Davidson guy knows there's other brands out there, maybe more efficient, lower priced, or higher performance. But he doesn't care. He wants that Harley. Same thing with the Gretsch guy. He wants that Gretsch." *Mike Lewis, Gretsch marketing manager*

INTO THE SEVENTH DECADE

The new partner appears to be doing only good things for Gretsch, with the guitars evidently better than they've ever been.

Guitarists continue to go for the sound and the look, whether it's Bono strumming a one-off green Irish Falcon, Chris Collingswood and Jody Porter in the wonderful Fountains Of Wayne with a new Anniversary and an old Gent, John Frusciante thrashing a Falcon on a couple of tracks on the Chili Peppers' *Californication*, or perhaps you in your latest cutting-edge covers band showing just what a Gretsch can do in the right hands.

In recent catalogues, Gretsch boasts about being in its "third century of instrument making". So what's the continuing attraction of Gretsch electric guitars a mere six decades on? Fred Gretsch III doesn't hesitate in his answer.

"If you want a one-word reply, it's cool. But in the end, it comes down to the music that you create with our instruments, music that you really can't create on anything else. There's the cool factor and there's the music factor – and I think the music comes first. The cool is just a nice plus."

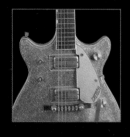

Reference
Section

HOW TO USE THE REFERENCE LISTING

The main Reference listing offers a simple, condensed format to convey a large amount of information about every Gretsch electric guitar model, and the following notes are intended to help you use this unique inventory.

The list covers all electric 'Spanish' guitars (in other words regular models rather than those played on the lap) issued by Gretsch between 1939 and 2004.

Each model is allocated to one of 26 distinctive body shapes, which we have called Styles. These are numbered and listed in the chronological order of their introduction. Corresponding body silhouettes are ranged along the bottom of each spread, or pair of pages; those that are shown on a particular spread in a darker shade relate to the accompanying text.

Under each style heading, the relevant models are listed in alphabetical sequence. The model numbers employed by Gretsch to denote differences are also included in the listings.

At the head of each entry is the model name (and number if applicable) in bold type. This is followed by a date or range of dates showing the production period of the instrument. These dates and any others in the Reference section are naturally as accurate as possible, but should still be considered approximate. As with any other guitar company, there is *no* guaranteed, foolproof method to pinpoint exact periods of Gretsch manufacture. All dating should be considered as a guide, not as gospel. Note that 'c' in front of a date stands for 'circa', meaning 'about'.

In italics, following the model name/number and production dates, is a brief, one-sentence identification of the guitar in question. This is intended to help you recognise a specific model at a glance. To do this we have noted the more obvious features that in combination are unique to that model.

For some guitars, usually those that exist in different versions, there may be a sentence below this, reading 'Similar to... except...'. This will refer to another model entry, and the accompanying description will list any major differences between the two.

The list of specification points, separated into groups, provides details of the model's features. In the order listed the points refer to:

- Neck, fingerboard; position markers; frets; location of truss-rod adjuster; headstock
- Body; finish
- Pickups
- Controls
- Pickguard
- Bridge, tailpiece
- Hardware plating finish
- Special features, if any

Note that some special order options were and are available on various models, but not all are recorded in the Reference listing.

Of course, not every model will need all eight points, and to avoid undue repetition we have considered a number of features to be common to all Gretsch guitars. They are:

- Glued-in neck unless stated
- Headstock with three tuners each side unless stated
- All controls on body front unless stated
- Side-mounted jack socket unless stated
- Metal bridge saddle(s) with wooden or metal base unless stated
- Nickel- or chrome-plated hardware unless stated

Some models were made in a number of variations, and where applicable these are listed, in italics, after the specification points. Any other general comments are also made here, in similar fashion.

Some entries consist only of a short listing, all in italics. This is usually because the model concerned is a reissue of, or a re-creation based on, an earlier guitar, and the text simply refers to the original instrument. Alternative name/number designations are also listed as separate, brief italicised entries. Reading 'See...', each refers to the appropriate main model(s).

All this information is designed to tell you more about your Gretsch guitar. By using the general history and illustrations earlier in this book and combining them with the knowledge you obtain from this Reference section, you should be able to build up a very full picture of your instrument and its pedigree.

GRETSCH ELECTRICS REFERENCE LISTING

BODY STYLES
Models are grouped in this listing under a series of headings that indicate one of 26 distinct body Styles. For instant reference, the Styles are illustrated in silhouette along the bottom of each pair of pages, numbered 1 to 26.

STYLE ONE (1939-58) USA
Non-cutaway large body

CLIPPER first version 1956-58 *One pickup, two controls, 21 frets.*
- Unbound rosewood fingerboard, dot markers; 21 frets; truss-rod adjuster at headstock.
- Hollow archtop bound body with two large f-holes; sunburst (6186), beige/grey (6187) or natural (6188).
- One single-coil pickup at neck.
- Two controls (volume, tone).
- Coloured plastic pickguard.
- Single-saddle wooden bridge, separate G-hole flat tailpiece.

Some examples in cream/grey (6187). Succeeded by one-cutaway second version, see listing under STYLE TWO.

CORVETTE hollow body version 1954-56 *One pickup, two controls, 20 frets.*
- Unbound rosewood fingerboard, dot markers; 20 frets; Electromatic on headstock.
- Hollow archtop bound body with two large f-holes; sunburst (6182) or natural (6183) (or gold – 6184 – from c1955).
- One single-coil pickup at neck.
- Two controls (volume, tone).
- Tortoiseshell plastic pickguard (coloured plastic on 6184).
- Single-saddle wooden bridge, separate trapeze tailpiece.

Previously known as ELECTROMATIC SPANISH second version, see separate listing.

ELECTRO II first version 1951-54 *Two pickups, three controls, 20 frets.*
- Bound rosewood fingerboard, block markers; 20 frets; Electromatic on headstock.
- Hollow archtop bound body with two large f-holes; sunburst (6187) or natural (6188).
- Two single-coil pickups.
- Three controls (two volume, one tone).
- Single-saddle wooden bridge, separate trapeze tailpiece.

ELECTROMATIC SPANISH first version 1939-42 *One pickup, two controls.*
- Hollow archtop body with two f-holes; sunburst.
- One single-coil pickup.
- Two controls (volume, tone).

No other information available.

ELECTROMATIC SPANISH second version 1949-54 *20 frets, one pickup, two controls.*
- Unbound rosewood fingerboard, dot markers; 20 frets; Electromatic on headstock.
- Hollow archtop bound body with two large f-holes; sunburst (6185; 6182 from c1952), or natural (6185N c1951-52; 6183 from c1952).
- One single-coil pickup at neck.
- Two controls (volume, tone).
- Tortoiseshell plastic pickguard.
- Single-saddle wooden bridge, separate trapeze tailpiece.

Known as CORVETTE hollow body version from c1954, see separate listing.

STYLE ONE (2001-03) Korea

HISTORIC SERIES SYNCHROMATIC JR 2001-03
See Style Two (Korea) HISTORIC SERIES THINLINE SYNCHROMATIC.

STYLE TWO (1951-81, 1995-current) USA
One rounded cutaway on large body

ANNIVERSARY one-pickup 1958-72
Anniversary on headstock, one pickup at neck.
- Unbound ebony fingerboard (rosewood from c1960), half-moon markers; 21 frets; truss-rod adjuster at headstock; model nameplate on headstock.
- Hollow archtop bound body with two large f-holes; sunburst (6124) or light/dark green (6125).

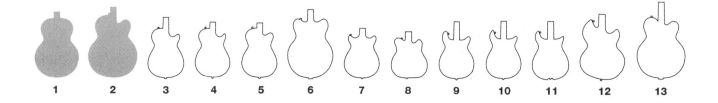

1   2   3   4   5   6   7   8   9   10   11   12   13

- One humbucker pickup at neck (one single-coil pickup from c1961).
- One control (volume) and one selector.
- Coloured plastic pickguard.
- Six-saddle bridge, separate G-hole flat tailpiece.
- Clip-on vibrato lever c1962-65.
Some examples with 22 frets.
Some examples in light/dark brown (6125) from c1963.

ANNIVERSARY two-pickup first version 1958-72 *Anniversary on headstock, two pickups.*

- Unbound (bound from c1962) ebony fingerboard (rosewood from c1960), half-moon markers; 21 frets (plus zero fret from c1968); truss-rod adjuster at headstock; model nameplate on headstock.
- Hollow archtop bound body with two large f-holes; sunburst (6117) or light/dark green (6118).
- Two humbucker pickups (two single-coil pickups from c1961).
- Three controls (all volume) and two selectors.
- Coloured plastic pickguard with Gretsch logo.
- Six-saddle bridge, separate G-hole flat tailpiece.
- Clip-on vibrato lever c1962-65.
Some examples with 20 or 22 frets.
Some examples in light/dark brown (6118) from c1963.
Also known as DOUBLE ANNIVERSARY.

ANNIVERSARY two-pickup second version 1972-74 *Two single-coil pickups, G-hole flat tailpiece.*
Similar to first version, except:
- Bound rosewood fingerboard, half-moon markers; 22 frets and zero fret; truss-rod adjuster at neck heel; no model nameplate on headstock.

- Hollow archtop bound body with two f-holes; sunburst (7560).

ANNIVERSARY two-pickup third version 1974-77 *Anniversary on pickguard, frame-type tailpiece.*
Similar to second version, except:
- Block markers.
- Three controls (two volume, one tone) and one selector.
- Coloured plastic pickguard with Anniversary logo.
- Six-saddle bridge, separate frame-type tailpiece.

ANNIVERSARY STEREO 1961-63
Model name on headstock, two close-spaced split-polepiece single-coil pickups.
Similar to ANNIVERSARY two-pickup first version, except:
- Sunburst (6111) or light/dark green (6112).
- Two split-polepiece single-coil pickups (close-spaced – one at neck, one in central position).
- Two controls (both volume) and three selectors.

'CAT'S-EYE CUSTOM' 1964-67 *'Cat's-Eye' soundholes.*
- Bound rosewood fingerboard, half-moon markers; 22 frets plus zero fret; truss-rod adjuster at headstock.
- Hollow archtop bound body with two 'cat's eye' soundholes; various colours (6117).
- Two single-coil pickups.
- Four controls (two volume, two tone) and one selector.
- Coloured plastic pickguard.
- Six-saddle bridge, separate G-hole flat tailpiece.
Some examples with 21 frets.

CHET ATKINS COUNTRY GENTLEMAN first version 1957-61
Chet Atkins Country Gentleman on headstock.
- Bound ebony fingerboard, half-moon markers; 22 frets (plus zero fret from c1959); truss-rod adjuster at headstock; model nameplate on headstock.
- Hollow archtop bound body with two fake f-holes; dark brown (6122).
- Two humbucker pickups.
- Three controls (all volume) and two selectors.
- Coloured plastic pickguard.
- Single-saddle bridge, separate vibrato tailpiece.
- Gold-plated hardware.
Some examples with f-holes.
Some examples with Chet Atkins logo on pickguard.
Succeeded by twin-cutaway second version, see listing under STYLE SIX.

CHET ATKINS HOLLOW BODY 6120 first version 1955-61 *Chet Atkins logo on pickguard, orange.*
- Bound rosewood fingerboard (ebony from c1958), engraved block markers (plain block from c1956; hump-top block from c1957; half-moon from c1958); 22 frets (plus zero fret from c1959); truss-rod adjuster at headstock; steer head on headstock (horseshoe from c1956).
- Hollow archtop bound body with two large f-holes and G-brand on front (no G-brand from c1957); orange (6120).
- Two single-coil pickups (two humbuckers from c1958).
- Four controls (three volume, one tone) and one selector (three controls – all volume – and two selectors from c1958).
- Coloured plastic pickguard with Chet Atkins logo.

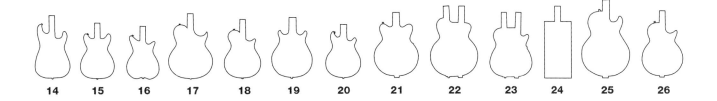

14   15   16   17   18   19   20   21   22   23   24   25   26

- Single-saddle bridge, separate vibrato tailpiece.
- Gold-plated hardware.

Some examples with 21 frets.
Some examples in red (6120).
Succeeded by twin-cutaway second version, see listing under STYLE SIX.

CHET ATKINS TENNESSEAN first version 1958-61 *Chet Atkins logo on pickguard, one humbucker pickup near bridge.*

- Unbound ebony fingerboard, half-moon markers; 22 frets (plus zero fret from c1959); truss-rod adjuster at headstock.
- Hollow archtop bound body with two large f-holes; dark red (6119).
- One humbucker pickup near bridge.
- One control (volume) and one selector.
- Coloured plastic pickguard with Chet Atkins logo.
- Single-saddle bridge, separate vibrato tailpiece.

Some examples with 21 frets.

CHET ATKINS TENNESSEAN second version 1961-72 *Chet Atkins Tennessean on pickguard, two single-coil pickups, fake f-holes.*

Similar to first version, except:

- Bound rosewood fingerboard; model nameplate on headstock (c1964-71).
- Hollow archtop bound body with two fake f-holes; dark red or dark brown (6119).
- Two single-coil pickups.
- Three controls (all volume) and three selectors.
- Coloured plastic pickguard with model name.

CHET ATKINS TENNESSEAN third version 1972-80 *Model name on pickguard, two single-coil pickups, f-holes.*

Similar to second version, except:

- Truss-rod adjuster at neck heel; no model nameplate on headstock.
- Hollow archtop bound body with two f-holes; dark red (7655).
- Three controls (all volume) and two selectors from c1978.
- Six-saddle bridge.

CLIPPER second version 1957-72
One single-coil pickup at neck, dot markers.

- Unbound rosewood fingerboard, dot markers; 21 frets; truss-rod adjuster on headstock.
- Hollow archtop bound body with two large f-holes; sunburst (6186), or natural (6187) c1958-59.
- One single-coil pickup at neck.
- Two controls (volume, tone) (located near body edge from c1967).
- Coloured plastic pickguard.
- Single-saddle wooden bridge, separate trapeze tailpiece.

Some examples with 22 frets, in cream/grey (6187) and separate G-hole flat tailpiece.
Succeeded non-cutaway first version, see listing under STYLE ONE.

CLIPPER third version 1972-75 *Two single-coil pickups, trapeze tailpiece.*

- Bound rosewood fingerboard, half-moon markers; 22 frets plus zero fret; truss-rod adjuster at neck heel.
- Hollow archtop bound body with two f-holes; sunburst/black (7555).
- Two single-coil pickups.
- Three controls (all volume) and two selectors.
- Coloured plastic pickguard.
- Six-saddle bridge, separate trapeze tailpiece.

CONVERTIBLE 1955-59 One pickup attached to elongated pickguard.

- Bound rosewood fingerboard (ebony from c1958), hump-top block markers (half-moon from c1958); 21 frets; truss-rod adjuster at headstock.
- Hollow archtop bound body with two large f-holes; cream/brown (6199).
- One single-coil pickup, attached to pickguard.
- Two controls (volume, tone) mounted on pickguard.
- Coloured elongated plastic pickguard.
- Single-saddle wooden bridge, separate G-hole flat tailpiece.
- Gold-plated hardware.

Some examples in sunburst.
Some examples in yellow/brown (6199) from c1958.
Known as SAL SALVADOR from c1959, see separate listing.

COUNTRY CLUB first version 1954-58 *Two single-coil pickups, G-hole flat tailpiece, gold-plated hardware.*

- Bound rosewood fingerboard, block markers (hump-top block from c1955); 21 frets; truss-rod adjuster at headstock.
- Hollow archtop bound body with two large f-holes; sunburst (6192), natural (6193) or green (6196).
- Two single-coil pickups.
- Four controls (three volume, one tone) and one selector.
- Tortoiseshell plastic pickguard (coloured plastic from c1955).
- Six-saddle bridge, separate G-hole flat tailpiece.
- Gold-plated hardware.

Some examples in light/dark grey (6196) and other colours.
Previously known as ELECTRO II second version, see separate listing.

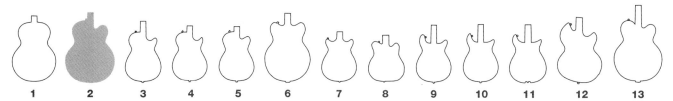

| 1 | 2 | 3 | 4 | 5 | 6 | 7 | 8 | 9 | 10 | 11 | 12 | 13 |

See **BODY STYLES** page 108

COUNTRY CLUB second version

1958-72 *Two humbucker pickups, G-hole flat tailpiece, gold-plated hardware.* Similar to first version, except:

- Bound ebony fingerboard, half-moon markers; 21 frets (plus zero fret from c1959).
- Two humbucker pickups.
- Three controls (all volume) and two selectors (three selectors from c1962; plus one string damper control c62-65).
- Pad on body back c1962-63.
- String damper and control c1962-65.

COUNTRY CLUB third version 1972-74 *Two humbucker pickups, G-hole flat tailpiece, gold-plated hardware, truss-rod adjuster at neck heel.*

Similar to second version, except:

- Truss-rod adjuster at neck heel.
- Hollow archtop bound body with two f-holes; sunburst (7575) or natural (7576).

COUNTRY CLUB fourth version

1974-81 *Country Club on nameplate over frame-type tailpiece.*
Similar to third version, except:

- Block markers; 22 frets.
- Natural (7576) or brown (7577) from c1977.
- Five controls (three volume, two tone) and one selector.
- Separate frame-type tailpiece with model nameplate overlay.

COUNTRY CLUB 1955 CUSTOM

6196-1955 1995-99 *Reissue based on 1955-period natural-finish original, but with bound ebony fingerboard. Also blue sunburst, green 1997-99.*

COUNTRY CLUB STEREO first

version 1958-60 *Two close-spaced split-polepiece humbucker pickups.*

- Bound ebony fingerboard, half-moon markers; 21 frets (plus zero fret from c1959); truss-rod adjuster at headstock.
- Hollow archtop bound body with two large f-holes; sunburst (6101), natural (6102) or green (6103).
- Two split-polepiece humbucker pickups (close-spaced – one at neck, one in central position).
- Two controls (both volume) and three selectors.
- Coloured plastic pickguard.
- Six-saddle bridge, separate G-hole flat tailpiece.
- Gold-plated hardware.

COUNTRY CLUB STEREO second

version 1960-65 *Two humbucker pickups, two controls and five selectors.*
Similar to first version, except:

- Two humbucker pickups.
- Two controls (both volume) and five selectors (plus one string damper control c1962-65).
- Pad on body back c1962-63.
- String damper and control c1962-65.

COUNTRY GENTLEMAN See CHET ATKINS COUNTRY GENTLEMAN first version listing.

DOUBLE ANNIVERSARY See ANNIVERSARY two-pickup listings.

ELECTRO II second version 1951-54 *Synchromatic on headstock, two single-coil pickups.*

- Bound rosewood fingerboard, block markers; 21 frets; truss-rod adjuster at body end of neck; Synchromatic on headstock.
- Hollow archtop bound body with two large f-holes; sunburst (6192) or natural (6193).

- Two single-coil pickups.
- Three controls (two volume, one tone) (four controls – two volume, two tone – from c1952; and one selector from c1954).
- Tortoiseshell plastic pickguard.
- Single-saddle wooden bridge (six-saddle bridge from c1952), separate harp-frame tailpiece or G-hole flat tailpiece.
- Gold-plated hardware.

Some examples with 19 frets.
Known as COUNTRY CLUB first version from c1954, see separate listing.

ELECTROMATIC 1951-54 *Electromatic on headstock, one or two single-coil pickups, trapeze tailpiece.*

- Bound rosewood fingerboard, block markers; 21 frets; Electromatic on headstock.
- Hollow archtop bound body with two large f-holes; sunburst (6190) or natural (6191).
- One single-coil pickup at neck.
- Two controls (volume, tone).
- Tortoiseshell plastic pickguard.
- Six-saddle bridge, separate trapeze tailpiece.

Some examples with two single-coil pickups (6189).
Known as STREAMLINER first version from c1954, see separate listing.

HOLLOW BODY See CHET ATKINS HOLLOW BODY first version listing.

NASHVILLE WESTERN 6120WCST

2004-current *Steer head on headstock, G-brand on body front, Nashville logo on pickguard.*

- Bound rosewood fingerboard, western motif block markers, 22 frets; truss-rod adjuster at headstock; steer head on headstock.

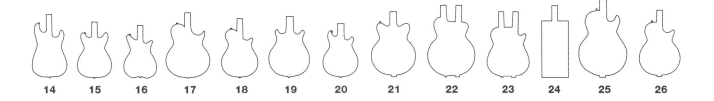

14	15	16	17	18	19	20	21	22	23	24	25	26

- Hollow archtop bound body with two large f-holes and G-brand on front; orange (6120WCST).
- Two single-coil pickups.
- Four controls (three volume, one tone) and one selector.
- Coloured plastic pickguard with Nashville logo.
- Single-saddle bridge, separate vibrato tailpiece.
- Gold-plated hardware (except vibrato tailpiece).

US Custom Shop limited production.

NASHVILLE 1955 CUSTOM 6120-1955 1995-99 *Reissue based on CHET ATKINS HOLLOW BODY (6120) 1955-period orange original, but with ebony fingerboard. Also black 1997-99. Also NASHVILLE 1955 CUSTOM WESTERN 6120W-1955 with western motif markers, G-brand on body front 1997-99.*

PROJECT-0-SONIC See COUNTRY CLUB STEREO and WHITE FALCON STEREO listings.

SAL SALVADOR 1959-67 *One pickup, elongated pickguard with or without controls.*

- Bound ebony fingerboard, half-moon markers (block from c1964); 21 frets (plus zero fret from c1960); truss-rod adjuster at headstock.
- Hollow archtop bound body with two large f-holes; sunburst (6199).
- One humbucker pickup (one single-coil from c1962) attached to pickguard (mounted on body from c1964).
- Two controls (volume, tone) mounted on pickguard (mounted on body from c1964).
- Coloured elongated plastic pickguard.
- Single-saddle wooden bridge, separate G-hole flat tailpiece.

- Gold-plated hardware.

Previously known as CONVERTIBLE, see separate listing.

STREAMLINER first version 1954-59
One pickup, bound fingerboard.

- Bound rosewood fingerboard, block markers (hump-top block from c1955); 21 frets; truss-rod adjuster at headstock; Electromatic on headstock until c1958.
- Hollow archtop bound body with two large f-holes; gold (6189), yellow/brown (6189), sunburst (6190) or natural (6191).
- One single-coil pickup at neck (one humbucker from c1958).
- Two controls (volume, tone) (volume plus one selector from c1958).
- Coloured plastic pickguard.
- Six-saddle bridge, separate G-hole flat tailpiece.

Previously known as ELECTROMATIC, see separate listing.

TENNESSEAN See CHET ATKINS TENNESSEAN listings.

VAN EPS seven-string first version 1968-72 *Van Eps on asymmetric headstock, seven strings.*

- Bound ebony fingerboard, half-moon markers; 21 frets plus zero fret; truss-rod adjuster at headstock; model nameplate on headstock; four and three tuners-per-side asymmetric headstock.
- Hollow archtop bound body with two large f-holes; sunburst (6079) or brown (6080).
- Two humbucker pickups.
- Three controls (all volume) and three selectors.
- Coloured plastic pickguard.
- Bar-frame 'Floating Sound' unit plus

single-saddle wooden bridge, separate G-hole flat tailpiece.
- Gold-plated hardware.

VAN EPS seven-string second version 1972-78 *Two humbucker pickups, asymmetric headstock, seven strings.*

Similar to first version, except:

- Truss-rod adjuster at neck heel; no model nameplate on headstock.
- Sunburst (7580), or brown (7581) c1972.
- Bar-frame 'Floating Sound' unit plus six-saddle bridge.

Some late examples with three controls (all volume) and two selectors; no 'Floating Sound' unit; single-saddle wooden bridge; chrome-plated hardware.

VAN EPS six-string 1968-72 *Van Eps on asymmetric headstock, six strings.*

Similar to VAN EPS seven-string first version, except:

- Three tuners-per-side asymmetric headstock.
- Sunburst (6081) or brown (6082).

WHITE FALCON first version 1955-62
Falcon logo on pickguard, hump-top block or half-moon markers.

- Bound ebony fingerboard, engraved hump-top block markers (half-moon from c1958); 21 frets (plus zero fret from c1959); truss-rod adjuster at headstock; vertical Gretsch logo on headstock (horizontal type plus model nameplate from c1958).
- Hollow archtop bound body with two large f-holes; white (6136).
- Two single-coil pickups (two humbucker pickups from c1958).
- Four controls (three volume, one tone) and one selector (three controls – all volume – and two selectors c1958-61;

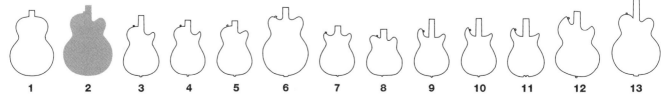

1   **2**   **3**   **4**   **5**   **6**   **7**   **8**   **9**   **10**   **11**   **12**   **13**

See **BODY STYLES** page 108

three controls – all volume – and three selectors, plus two string damper controls from c1961.
- Coloured plastic pickguard with falcon logo.
- Six-saddle bridge, separate G-logo tubular frame-type tailpiece.
- Gold-plated hardware.
- Pad on body back from c1961.
- Double string damper and two controls from c1961.

Some examples with 22 frets.
Some examples in black.
Some examples with optional separate vibrato tailpiece.
Succeeded by twin-cutaway second version, see listing under STYLE SIX.

WHITE FALCON fourth version 1974-78 *Falcon logo on pickguard, block markers.*
- Bound ebony fingerboard, block markers; 21 frets plus zero fret; truss-rod adjuster at neck heel.
- Hollow archtop bound body with two f-holes; white (7593).
- Two humbucker pickups.
- Three controls (all volume) and two selectors.
- Coloured plastic pickguard with falcon logo.
- Six-saddle bridge, separate vibrato tailpiece.
- Gold-plated hardware.

Some examples with separate frame-type tailpiece.

WHITE FALCON STEREO first version 1958-59 *Falcon logo on pickguard, two close-spaced split-polepiece humbucker pickups.*
- Bound ebony fingerboard, engraved hump-top block markers (half-moon from c1958); 21 frets (plus zero fret from c1959); truss-rod adjuster at

headstock; vertical Gretsch logo on headstock (horizontal type plus model nameplate from c1958).
- Hollow archtop bound body with two large f-holes; white (6137).
- Two split-polepiece humbucker pickups (close-spaced – one at neck, one in central position).
- Two controls (both volume) and three selectors.
- Coloured plastic pickguard with falcon logo.
- Six-saddle bridge, separate G-logo tubular frame-type tailpiece.
- Gold-plated hardware.

Some examples with 22 frets.
Some examples with optional separate vibrato tailpiece.

WHITE FALCON STEREO second version 1959-62 *Falcon logo on pickguard, two controls and five selectors.* Similar to first version, except:
- Two humbucker pickups.
- Two controls (both volume) and five selectors (plus two string damper controls from c1961).
- Pad on body back from c1961.
- Double string damper and two controls from c1961.

Succeeded by twin-cutaway third version, see listing under STYLE SIX.

WHITE FALCON STEREO fifth version 1974-78. *Falcon logo on pickguard, two controls and five selectors, block markers.*
- Bound ebony fingerboard, block markers; 21 frets plus zero fret; truss-rod adjuster at neck heel.
- Hollow archtop bound body with two f-holes; white (7593).
- Two humbucker pickups.
- Two controls (both volume) and five selectors.

- Coloured plastic pickguard with falcon logo.
- Six-saddle bridge, separate vibrato tailpiece.
- Gold-plated hardware.

WHITE FALCON 1955 CUSTOM 6136-1955 1995-99 *Reissue based on 1955-period original, but with 22 frets as standard.*

WHITE FALCON 6136CST 2004-current *Falcon logo on pickguard, two single-coil pickups.*
- Bound ebony fingerboard, engraved hump-top block markers, 21 frets; truss-rod adjuster at headstock; vertical Gretsch logo on headstock.
- Hollow archtop bound body with two large f-holes; white (6136CST).
- Two single-coil pickups.
- Four controls (three volume, one tone) and one selector.
- Coloured plastic pickguard with falcon logo.
- Six-saddle bridge, separate G-logo tubular frame-type tailpiece.
- Gold-plated hardware

US Custom Shop limited production.

STYLE TWO (1989-current) Japan
One rounded cutaway on large body

ANNIVERSARY two-pickup 1993-current *Anniversary 1883-1993 on headstock, two pickups.*
- Bound ebony fingerboard (unbound from c2003), half-moon markers; 22 frets; truss-rod adjuster at headstock; model nameplate on headstock.
- Hollow archtop bound body with two large f-holes; light/dark green (6118).
- Two humbucker pickups.

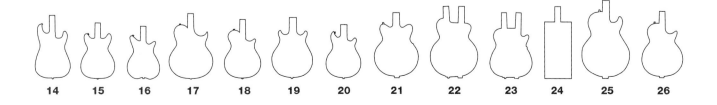

14   15   16   17   18   19   20   21   22   23   24   25   26

- Three controls (all volume) and two selectors.
- Coloured plastic pickguard.
- Six-saddle bridge, separate G-hole flat tailpiece.

Also sunburst (6117) 1993-98.
Also ANNIVERSARY HT 6117HT with two single-coil pickups from c2003.
Also ANNIVERSARY HT 6117THT with two single-coil pickups, separate vibrato tailpiece from c2004.
Also ANNIVERSARY 6118T with separate vibrato tailpiece from c2003.

ANNIVERSARY 6118T-120 2003-

current *Anniversary 1883-2003 on headstock, yellow body front, vibrato tailpiece.*
Similar to ANNIVERSARY two-pickup, except:
- Unbound ebony fingerboard.
- Yellow front on body.
- Anniversary 1883-2003 on headstock.
- Single-saddle bridge, separate vibrato tailpiece.

ANNIVERSARY one-pickup 1993-98

Anniversary 1883-1993 on headstock, one pickup.
Similar to ANNIVERSARY two-pickup, except:
- Sunburst (6124), light/dark green (6125).
- One humbucker pickup.
- One control (volume) and one selector.

BLACK FALCON 6136BK 1992-98,

2003-current *Falcon logo on pickguard, 22 frets, G-logo tubular frame-type tailpiece, black.*
Similar to WHITE FALCON 6136, except:
- Black (6136BK).
Also BLACK FALCON 6136TBK with separate vibrato tailpiece from c2004.

BLACK FALCON 7593BK 1992-98,

2003-current *Falcon logo on pickguard, 22 frets, vibrato tailpiece, black.*
Similar to WHITE FALCON 7593, except:
- Black (7593BK)

BRIAN SETZER See NASHVILLE

BRIAN SETZER 6120SSU listing.

COUNTRY CLASSIC I 6122S 1989-

2003 *Country Classic I on headstock and pickguard.*
- Bound ebony fingerboard, half-moon markers; 22 frets; truss-rod adjuster at headstock; model nameplate on headstock.
- Hollow archtop bound body with two f-holes; dark brown (6122S).
- Two humbucker pickups.
- Four controls (three volume, one tone) and one selector.
- Coloured plastic pickguard with model name.
- Six-saddle bridge, separate vibrato tailpiece.
- Gold-plated hardware.

COUNTRY CLASSIC 6122-1958 1997-

current *Model nameplate on headstock.*
Similar to COUNTRY CLASSIC I 6122S, except:
- Model nameplate on headstock; shorter scale length.
- Two fake f-holes.
- Three controls (all volume) and two selectors.
- Single-saddle bridge.
- Gold-plated hardware (except vibrato tailpiece).

COUNTRY CLUB 6196 2001-current

Two single-coil pickups, gold-plated hardware.
- Bound ebony or rosewood fingerboard, block or hump-top block

markers, 22 frets; truss-rod adjuster at headstock.
- Hollow archtop bound body with two large f-holes; green (6196).
- Two single-coil pickups.
- Four controls (three volume, one tone) and one selector.
- Coloured plastic pickguard.
- Six-saddle bridge, separate G-hole flat tailpiece.
- Gold-plated hardware.

Also sunburst (6192) from c2003; some examples with half-moon markers.
Also natural (6193) from c2003; some examples with half-moon markers.

COUNTRY CLUB 6196T 2004-current

Three selectors, two humbuckers.
Similar to COUNTRY CLUB 6196, except:
- Bound ebony fingerboard, half-moon markers.
- Amber (6193T), green (6196T)
- Two humbucker pickups.
- Three controls (all volume) and three selectors.
- Separate vibrato tailpiece.

DUANE EDDY 6120DE 1997-2003

Duane Eddy signature on truss-rod cover and pickguard.
Similar to NASHVILLE 6120, except:
- Bound ebony fingerboard, hump-top block markers; Duane Eddy signature on truss-rod cover; brass nut.
- Blackburst (6120DE) or orange (6120DEO).
- Two single-coil pickups.
- Coloured plastic pickguard with Duane Eddy signature.
- Gold-plated hardware (except vibrato tailpiece).

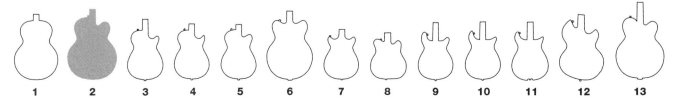

1   2   3   4   5   6   7   8   9   10   11   12   13

See **BODY STYLES** page 108

NASHVILLE BRIAN SETZER

6120SSU 1993-current *Brian Setzer signature on pickguard.*
Similar to NASHVILLE 6120-1960, except:
* 22 frets with NO zero fret; Brian Setzer on truss-rod cover.
* Two optional dice-style control knobs.
* Coloured plastic pickguard with Brian Setzer signature and model name.

Also vintage-style cellulose lacquer (6120SSL).
Also green (6120SSUGR).
Also vintage orange (6120SSLVO) c2004.

NASHVILLE BRIAN SETZER HOT

ROD 6120SH 1999-current *Brian Setzer Hot Rod on headstock, one control.*
Similar to NASHVILLE 6120, except:
* Half-moon markers; Brian Setzer Hot Rod on headstock.
* Blue, orange, purple, red.
* One volume control and one selector.
* Hot Rod logo on pickguard.
* Chrome-plated hardware.

Also black from c2002.
Also lime gold from c2004.

NASHVILLE CLASSIC 6122-1959

2003-current *Model nameplate on headstock.*
* Bound ebony fingerboard, half-moon markers, 22 frets; truss-rod adjuster at headstock; model nameplate on headstock.
* Hollow archtop bound body with two fake f-holes; dark brown (6122-1959).
* Two humbucker pickups (differing types).
* Three controls (two volume, one tone) and one selector.
* Coloured plastic pickguard.
* Single-saddle bridge, separate vibrato tailpiece.
* Gold-plated hardware.

NASHVILLE DYNASONIC 6120DS

2003-current *Horseshoe on headstock, block markers, two single-coil pickups.*
Similar to NASHVILLE 6120, except:
* Two single-coil pickups.
* Single-saddle bridge.
* Gold-plated hardware (except vibrato tailpiece).

NASHVILLE DYNASONIC WESTERN

6120DSW 2003-current *Steer head on headstock,, G-brand on body front, two single-coil pickups.*
Similar to NASHVILLE WESTERN 6120W, except:
* Steer head on headstock.
* G-brand on orange body front.
* Two single-coil pickups.
* Single-saddle bridge.
* Gold-plated hardware (except vibrato tailpiece).

NASHVILLE GOLDEN ANNIVERSARY

6120GA 2004-current *Gold body front, half moon markers.*
Similar to NASHVILLE 6120-1960, except:
* 22 frets with NO zero fret.
* Gold body front.
* Single-saddle bridge.

NASHVILLE KEITH SCOTT 6120KS

1999-current *Keith Scott signature on truss-rod cover and pickguard, gold front.*
Similar to NASHVILLE 6120, except:
* Bound ebony fingerboard, hump-top block markers; Keith Scott signature on truss-rod cover.
* Gold body front.
* Two single-coil pickups.
* Coloured plastic pickguard with Keith Scott signature and model name.

NASHVILLE WESTERN 6120W 1989-

2003 *Western motif block markers, G-logo on body front.*
Similar to NASHVILLE, except:
* Western motif block markers.
* Body G-logo on front; orange (6120W).
* Coloured plastic pickguard with Nashville logo.

NASHVILLE WESTERN 6120W-1957

2001-current *Clear plastic pickguard, two differing type single-coil pickups.*
Similar to NASHVILLE DYNASONIC WESTERN 6120DSW, except:
* Clear plastic pickguard with Nashville logo.
* Two single-coil pickups (differing types).

Based on Eddie Cochran's personally modified 1950s 6120 model.

NASHVILLE 6120 1989-current

Horseshoe on headstock, block markers.
* Bound rosewood fingerboard, block markers; 22 frets; truss-rod adjuster at headstock; horseshoe on headstock.
* Hollow archtop bound body with two large f-holes; orange (6120).
* Two humbucker pickups.
* Four controls (three volume, one tone) and one selector (three controls, all volume, and two selectors from c2003).
* Coloured plastic pickguard.
* Six-saddle bridge, separate vibrato tailpiece.
* Gold-plated hardware.

Also blue sunburst (6120BS) from c1992.
Also green (6120GR) from c1993.
Also tiger maple (6120TM) from c1993.
Also black (6120BK) from c2003.
Also amber (6120AM) from c2003.

NASHVILLE 6120-1960 1992-current

Horseshoe on headstock, half-moon

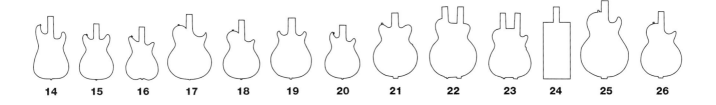

14   15   16   17   18   19   20   21   22   23   24   25   26

markers, zero fret.
Similar to NASHVILLE 6120, except:
* Bound ebony fingerboard, half-moon markers; 22 frets plus zero fret.
* Three controls (all volume) and two selectors.

RANCHER 6022CV 1992-99 *Steer head on headstock, triangular soundhole, one pickup.*
* Bound ebony fingerboard, block markers; 20 frets; truss-rod adjuster at headstock; steer head on headstock.
* Hollow flat-top bound body with triangular soundhole; orange (6022CV).
* One single-coil pickup at neck.
* Two controls (volume, tone) mounted on body side.
* Six-saddle bridge, separate vibrato tailpiece.

SILVER FALCON 6136SL 1995-current *Falcon logo on pickguard, 22 frets, G-logo tubular frame-type tailpiece, black, chrome-plated hardware.*
Similar to WHITE FALCON 6136, except:
* Black (6136SL).
* Chrome-plated hardware.
Also SILVER FALCON 6136TSL with separate vibrato tailpiece from c2004.

SYNCHROMATIC 400MCV 1992-2001 *Synchromatic on headstock, vibrato tailpiece.*
* Bound ebony fingerboard, split hump-top block markers; 20 frets; truss-rod adjuster at headstock; Synchromatic on headstock.
* Hollow archtop bound body with two 'cat's-eye' soundholes; natural.
* One humbucker pickup at neck.
* Two controls (volume, tone) mounted on pickguard.
* Coloured and elongated plastic pickguard.

* Six-saddle bridge, separate vibrato tailpiece.
* Gold-plated hardware.
Also sunburst (400CV) 1994-2002.

SYNCHROMATIC 6040MC-SS 1994-current *Synchromatic on headstock, harp-frame tailpiece.*
Similar to SYNCHROMATIC 400MCV, except:
* Single-saddle wooden bridge, separate harp-frame tailpiece.

TENNESSEE ROSE 6119 1989-current *Tennessee Rose on pickguard, f-holes.*
* Bound rosewood fingerboard, half-moon markers; 22 frets; truss-rod adjuster at headstock.
* Hollow archtop bound body with two f-holes; dark red (6119).
* Two humbucker pickups.
* Four controls (three volume, one tone) and one selector.
* Coloured plastic pickguard with model name.
* Six-saddle bridge, separate vibrato tailpiece.

TENNESSEE ROSE 6119-1962FT 1993-current *Tennessee Rose on pickguard, fake f-holes, zero fret.*
Similar to TENNESSEE ROSE 6119, except:
* 22 frets plus zero fret.
* Hollow archtop bound body with two fake f-holes; brown (6119-1962).
* Three controls (all volume) and three selectors.
* Single-saddle bridge.

TENNESSEE ROSE 6119-1962HT 1999-current *Tennessee Rose on pickguard, two single-coil pickups.*
Similar to TENNESSEE ROSE 6119-

1962, except:
* Two single-coil pickups

TENNESSEE SPECIAL 6119SP 2003-current *Unbound ebony fingerboard, black plastic pickguard.*
* Unbound ebony fingerboard, half-moon markers, 22 frets plus zero fret; truss-rod adjuster at headstock.
* Hollow archtop bound body with two large f-holes; dark red.
* Two humbucker pickups.
* Three controls (all volume) and two selectors.
* Black plastic pickguard.
* Single-saddle bridge, separate vibrato tailpiece.

WHITE FALCON 6136 1989-current *Falcon logo on pickguard, 22 frets, G-logo tubular frame-type tailpiece, white.*
* Bound ebony fingerboard, hump-top block markers; 22 frets; truss-rod adjuster at headstock; vertical Gretsch logo on headstock.
* Hollow archtop bound body with two large f-holes; white (6136).
* Two humbucker pickups.
* Four controls (three volume, one tone) and one selector (three controls, all volume, and two selectors from c2003).
* Coloured plastic pickguard with falcon logo.
* Six-saddle bridge, separate G-logo tubular frame-type tailpiece.
* Gold-plated hardware.
Some early examples with block markers, horizontal Gretsch logo on headstock, two f-holes.
Also WHITE FALCON 6136T with separate vibrato tailpiece from c2004.

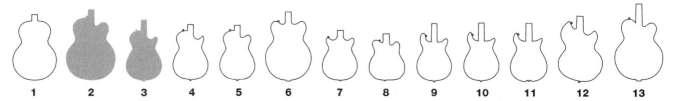

1   2   3   4   5   6   7   8   9   10   11   12   13

See **BODY STYLES** page 108

WHITE FALCON STEPHEN STILLS

6136-1958 2000-current *Stephen Stills signature on fingerboard.*
Similar to WHITE FALCON 6136, except:

- Half-moon markers; horizontal Gretsch logo on headstock; Stephen Stills signature on fingerboard.
- Aged white (6136-1958).
- Three controls (all volume) and two selectors.
- No pickguard.
- Separate vibrato tailpiece.

WHITE FALCON 7593 1989-current

Falcon logo on pickguard, 22 frets, vibrato tailpiece, white.
Similar to WHITE FALCON 6136, except:

- Block markers; horizontal Gretsch logo on headstock.
- Two f-holes; white (7593).
- Separate vibrato tailpiece.

STYLE TWO (1999-2003) Korea

One rounded cutaway on large body

ELECTROMATIC HOLLOW BODY

2004-current *Electromatic down headstock, black plastic pickguard.*

- Bound rosewood fingerboard, half-moon markers, 22 frets; truss-rod adjuster at headstock; Electromatic down headstock.
- Hollow archtop bound body with two large f-holes; black (5125), silver sparkle front (5126), light blue front (5127), gold sparkle front (5128), red front (5129).
- Two single-coil pickups.
- Four controls (three volume, one tone) and one selector.
- Black plastic pickguard.
- Six-saddle bridge, separate vibrato tailpiece.

HISTORIC SERIES STREAMLINER

1999-2003 *Historic Series on truss-rod cover, 'arrow-through-G' on headstock, two cat's-eye soundholes, six-saddle bridge, three controls.*

- Bound rosewood fingerboard, half-moon markers, 22 frets; truss-rod adjuster at headstock; Historic Series on truss-rod cover, 'arrow-through-G' on headstock.
- Hollow archtop bound body with two cat's-eye soundholes; red (3150), black (3151).
- Two single-coil pickups.
- Three controls (two volume, one tone) and one selector.
- Tortoiseshell plastic pickguard.
- Six-saddle bridge, separate G-hole flat tailpiece.

Also with separate vibrato tailpiece, gold-plated hardware; red (3155), white (3156).

HISTORIC SERIES SYNCHROMATIC

1999-2003 *Historic Series on truss-rod cover, 'arrow-through-G' on headstock, two cat's-eye soundholes, single-saddle wooden bridge, four controls.*

- Bound rosewood fingerboard, half-moon markers, 22 frets; truss-rod adjuster at headstock; Historic Series on truss-rod cover, 'arrow-through-G' on headstock.
- Hollow archtop bound body with two cat's-eye soundholes; sunburst (3110).
- Two single-coil pickups.
- Four controls (two volume, two tone) and one selector.
- Tortoiseshell plastic pickguard.
- Single-saddle wooden bridge, separate G-hole flat tailpiece.
- Gold-plated hardware.

HISTORIC SERIES THINLINE

SYNCHROMATIC 1999-2003 *Historic Series on truss-rod cover, 'arrow-through-G' on headstock, two bound cat's-eye soundholes, six-saddle bridge, three controls.*

- Bound rosewood fingerboard, half-moon markers, 22 frets; truss-rod adjuster at headstock; Historic Series on truss-rod cover, 'arrow-through-G' on headstock.
- Hollow archtop bound body with two bound cat's-eye soundholes; orange (3140), black (3141).
- Two single-coil pickups.
- Three controls (two volume, one tone) and one selector.
- Tortoiseshell plastic pickguard.
- Six-saddle bridge, separate G-hole flat tailpiece.
- Chrome-plated hardware.

Also HISTORIC SERIES SYNCHROMATIC JR with one single-coil pickup, gold body front (3967) 2001-03. Also HISTORIC SERIES SYNCHROMATIC JR with one single-coil pickup, non-cutaway body, tobacco sunburst (3900), vintage sunburst (3905) 2001-03.

STYLE THREE (1953-79) USA

One semi-pointed cutaway on small body

CHET ATKINS SOLID BODY first

version 1955-61 *Chet Atkins logo on pickguard, single-saddle bridge.*

- Bound rosewood fingerboard (ebony from c1958), engraved block markers (plain block from c1956; hump-top block from c1957; half-moon from c1958); 22 frets (plus zero fret from c1959); truss-rod adjuster at headstock; steer head on headstock (horseshoe from c1956).

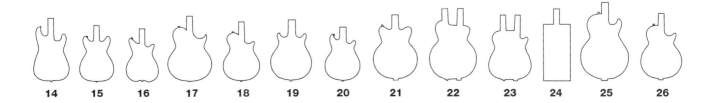

| 14 | 15 | 16 | 17 | 18 | 19 | 20 | 21 | 22 | 23 | 24 | 25 | 26 |

- Semi-solid bound body with G-brand on front (no G-brand from c1957); studded leather around sides (c1954-56); orange front (6121).
- Two single-coil pickups (two humbucker pickups from c1958).
- Four controls (three volume, one tone) and one selector (three controls – all volume – and two selectors from c1958).
- Coloured plastic pickguard with Chet Atkins logo.
- Single-saddle bridge, separate vibrato tailpiece.
- Gold-plated hardware.

Succeeded by twin-cutaway second version, see listing under STYLE SEVEN.

COUNTRY ROC 1974-79 *Orange body front, five controls and one selector, G-brand on body front.*

- Bound ebony fingerboard, western motif block markers; 22 frets plus zero fret; truss-rod adjuster at neck heel; horseshoe on headstock.
- Semi-solid bound body with G-brand on front; studded leather around sides; orange front (7620).
- Two humbucker pickups.
- Five controls (three volume, two tone) and one selector.
- Coloured plastic pickguard.
- Six-saddle bridge, separate G-hole tailpiece with western-style belt buckle.
- Gold-plated hardware.

DUO JET first version 1953-61 *Black body front.*

- Bound rosewood fingerboard, block markers (hump-top block from c1957; half-moon from c1958); 22 frets (plus zero fret from c1959); truss-rod adjuster at headstock.
- Semi-solid bound body; black front (6128).

- Two single-coil pickups (two humbucker pickups from c1958).
- Four controls (three volume, one tone) and one selector (three controls – all volume – and two selectors from c1958).
- Coloured plastic pickguard.
- Six-saddle bridge, separate G-hole flat tailpiece or vibrato tailpiece.

Some examples with green body-front and gold-plated hardware (6128).
Succeeded by twin-cutaway second version, see listing under STYLE SEVEN.

JET FIRE BIRD first version 1955-61
Red body front.
Similar to DUO JET first version, except:
- Black with red body front (6131).

Some examples with 21 frets.
Succeeded by twin-cutaway second version, see listing under STYLE SEVEN.

ROC II 1973-75 *Dark red, all controls on elliptical plate.*

- Bound ebony fingerboard, half-moon markers; 22 frets plus zero fret; truss-rod adjuster at neck heel.
- Solid bound body; dark red (7621).
- Two humbucker pickups.
- Four controls (two volume, treble boost, distortion) and two selectors, all on elliptical plate; active circuit.
- Six-saddle bridge/tailpiece.

ROC JET first version 1969-72 *Roc Jet on headstock.*

- Bound ebony fingerboard, half-moon markers; 22 frets plus zero fret; truss-rod adjuster at headstock; model nameplate on headstock.
- Semi-solid bound body; orange front (6127) or black front (6130).
- Two humbucker pickups.
- Coloured plastic pickguard.
- Five controls (three volume, two tone) and one selector.

- Six-saddle bridge, separate G-hole flat tailpiece.

ROC JET second version 1972-79
Various colour body fronts, truss-rod adjuster at neck heel, chrome-plated hardware.
Similar to first version, except:
- Bound rosewood fingerboard from c1977; truss-rod adjuster at neck heel; no model nameplate on headstock.
- Black front (7610) (7611 from c1977), orange front (7611) c1972-74, red front (7612) c1972-77, or brown front (7613) c1972-77.
- Six-saddle wrapover bridge/tailpiece from c1977.

ROUND UP 1954-59 *Orange body front, four controls and one selector, steer head logo on pickguard.*

- Bound rosewood fingerboard, engraved block markers; 22 frets; truss-rod adjuster at headstock; steer head on headstock.
- Semi-solid bound body with G-brand on front; studded leather around sides; orange front (6130).
- Two single-coil pickups.
- Four controls (three volume, one tone) and one selector.
- Tortoiseshell or coloured plastic pickguard with steer head logo.
- Six-saddle bridge, separate G-hole flat tailpiece with western-style belt buckle.
- Gold-plated hardware.

SILVER JET first version 1954-61
Silver sparkle body front.
Similar to DUO JET first version, except:
- Silver sparkle body-front (6129).

Succeeded by twin-cutaway second version, see listing under STYLE SEVEN.

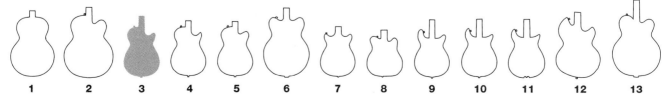

1   2   3   4   5   6   7   8   9   10   11   12   13

See **BODY STYLES** page 108

WHITE PENGUIN first version 1955-61 *Penguin logo on pickguard.*
- Bound ebony fingerboard, engraved hump-top block markers (half-moon from c1958); 22 frets; truss-rod adjuster at headstock; vertical Gretsch logo on headstock (horizontal type from c1958).
- Semi-solid bound body; white (6134).
- Two single-coil pickups (two humbucker pickups from c1958).
- Four controls (three volume, one tone) and one selector (three controls – all volume – and two selectors from c1958).
- Coloured plastic pickguard with penguin logo.
- Six-saddle bridge, separate G-logo tubular frame tailpiece.
- Gold-plated hardware.
- Metal arm-rest.

Some examples in black and white, or with gold sparkle body front.
Some examples without metal arm-rest.
Succeeded by twin-cutaway second version, see listing under STYLE SEVEN.

STYLE THREE (1989-current)
Japan

One semi-pointed cutaway on small body

BLACK PENGUIN 6134B 2003-current *Black, penguin logo on pickguard.*
Similar to WHITE PENGUIN, except:
- Black (6134B).

DUO JET 6128 1989-current *Black body front, two humbucker pickups.*
- Bound rosewood fingerboard, hump-top block markers; 22 frets; truss-rod adjuster at headstock; horseshoe on headstock.
- Semi-solid bound body; black front (6128).

- Two humbucker pickups.
- Four controls (three volume, one tone) and one selector (three controls, all volume, and two selectors from c2003).
- Coloured plastic pickguard
- Six-saddle bridge, separate G-hole flat tailpiece.
Also DUO JET 6128T with separate vibrato tailpiece from c1994.

DUO JET 6128-1957 1994-current *Black body front, two single-coil pickups.*
Similar to DUO JET 6128, except:
- No horseshoe on headstock.
- Two single-coil pickups.
Also DUO JET 6128T-1957 with separate vibrato tailpiece.
Also DUO JET SPECIAL 6128TSP with single-saddle bridge, separate vibrato tailpiece from 2004.

ELLIOT EASTON 6128TEE 2000-current *Elliot Easton signature on truss-rod cover and pickguard.*
Similar to DUO JET 6128, except:
- Bound ebony fingerboard, half-moon markers; Elliot Easton signature on truss-rod cover; longer scale length.
- Green body front (6128TEE), red body front (6128TREE), black body front (6128TBEE).
- Three controls (all volume) and two selectors.
- Coloured plastic pickguard with Elliot Easton signature.
- Separate vibrato tailpiece.
- Gold-plated hardware.

JET FIREBIRD 1989-current *Red body front, two humbucker pickups.*
Similar to DUO JET 6128, except:
- Red body front (6131).
- Gold-plated hardware (chrome-plated from c2002).

Also JET FIREBIRD 6131T with separate vibrato tailpiece from c2004.

NEW JET 6114 2002-2003 *Flame maple body front, two pickups with plain black tops.*
- Bound ebony fingerboard, hump-top block markers, 22 frets; truss-rod adjuster at headstock.
- Semi-solid bound body; flame maple front in black, natural, red.
- Two humbucker pickups.
- Four controls (three volume, one tone) and one selector.
- Coloured plastic pickguard.
- Six-saddle bridge, separate G-hole flat tailpiece.

ROUND UP 6121 1989-2003 *G-logo on orange body front, two humbucker pickups.*
Similar to DUO JET 6128, except:
- Western motif block markers; horseshoe on headstock.
- G-logo on orange body front (6121).
- Separate vibrato tailpiece,
- Gold-plated hardware.

ROUND UP 6121W 2003-current *Steer head on headstock, G-brand on body front.*
Similar to ROUND UP 6121, except:
- Steer head on headstock.
- G-brand on body front.
- Two single-coil pickups.
- Single-saddle bridge.
- Gold-plated hardware (except vibrato tailpiece).

SILVER JET 6129 1989-current *Silver sparkle body front, two humbucker pickups.*
Similar to DUO JET 6128, except:
- Silver sparkle body front (6129).
Also SILVER JET 6129T with separate vibrato tailpiece from c1994.

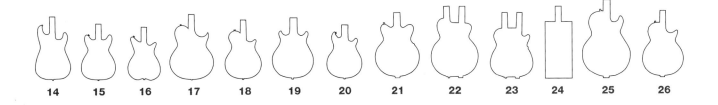

14   15   16   17   18   19   20   21   22   23   24   25   26

SILVER JET 6129-1957 1994-current
Silver sparkle body front, two single-coil pickups.
Similar to DUO JET 6128, except:
- No horseshoe on headstock.
- Silver sparkle body front.
- Two single-coil pickups.
Also SILVER JET 6129T-1957 with separate vibrato tailpiece.

SPARKLE JET 6129T 1995-current
Various colour sparkle (NOT silver) or blue pearl body fronts, two humbucker pickups.
Similar to DUO JET 6128, except:
- Black sparkle (1995-2003), champagne sparkle (1995-2003), red sparkle (1995-2003), gold sparkle, green sparkle, blue pearl body front.
- Separate vibrato tailpiece.

SPARKLE JET 6129-1957 1996-2002
Various colour sparkle (NOT silver) body fronts, two single-coil pickups.
Similar to DUO JET 6128, except:
- No horseshoe on headstock.
- Gold sparkle, green sparkle body front.
- Two single-coil pickups.
- Separate vibrato tailpiece.

WHITE PENGUIN 1993-94, 2003-current
White, penguin logo on pickguard.
- Bound ebony fingerboard, feather motif hump-top block markers; 22 frets; truss-rod adjuster at headstock; vertical Gretsch logo on headstock.
- Semi-solid bound body; white (6134).
- Two single-coil pickups.
- Four controls (three volume, one tone) and one selector.
- Coloured plastic pickguard with penguin logo.
- Six-saddle bridge, separate G-logo tubular frame tailpiece.
- Gold-plated hardware.

STYLE THREE (2000-current) Korea

ELECTROMATIC ELLIOT EASTON
2004-current Small Electromatic logo on headstock, Elliot Easton on truss-rod cover.
- Bound rosewood fingerboard, half-moon markers, 22 frets; truss-rod adjuster at headstock; Elliot Easton on truss-rod cover; small Electromatic logo on headstock.
- Semi-solid bound body; green front (5570).
- Two humbucker pickups.
- Three controls (all volume) and two selectors.
- Coloured plastic pickguard.
- Six-saddle bridge, separate vibrato tailpiece.
- Gold-plated hardware.
See also SYNCHROMATIC ELLIOT EASTON.

ELECTROMATIC JET BARITONE
2004-current Small Electromatic logo on headstock, extended scale length neck.
- Extended scale length neck, unbound rosewood fingerboard, dot markers, 22 frets; truss-rod adjuster at headstock; small Electromatic logo on headstock.
- Semi-solid bound body; black sparkle front (5265).
- Two humbucker pickups.
- Two controls (one volume, one tone) and one selector.
- Coloured plastic pickguard.
- Six-saddle bridge, separate vibrato tailpiece.
See also SYNCHROMATIC JET BARITONE.

ELECTROMATIC JET CLUB 2000-2003
Electromatic across headstock, block markers.
- Bolt-on neck with unbound rosewood fingerboard, block markers, 22 frets; truss-rod adjuster at headstock; Gretsch on truss-rod cover; Electromatic across headstock.
- Solid unbound body; sunburst (2403).
- Two humbucker pickups.
- Four controls (two volume, two tone) and one selector.
- Gretsch on coloured plastic pickguard.
- Six-saddle bridge, separate bar tailpiece.
Some examples with Electromatic by Gretsch across headstock.
See also SYNCHROMATIC JET CLUB.

ELECTROMATIC JET PRO 2000-2003
Electromatic across headstock, crown markers.
Similar to ELECTROMATIC JET CLUB, except:
- Glued-in neck, crown position markers.
- Figured front; sunburst (2504).
Also with separate vibrato tailpiece (2554).
See also SYNCHROMATIC JET PRO.

ELECTROMATIC JET SPARKLE 2000-2003
Electromatic across headstock, bound body.
- Bolt-on neck with unbound rosewood fingerboard, dot markers, 22 frets; truss-rod adjuster at headstock; Gretsch on truss-rod cover; Electromatic across headstock.
- Semi-solid bound body; black (2610), black sparkle front (2615), silver sparkle front (2616), blue sparkle front (2617), gold sparkle front (2618), red sparkle front (2619).
- Two humbucker pickups.
- Four controls (three volume, one tone) and one selector.
- Six-saddle wrapover bridge/tailpiece.
Some examples with Electromatic by Gretsch across headstock.
See also SYNCHROMATIC SPARKLE JET.

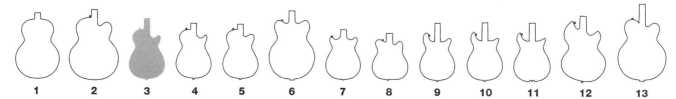

| 1 | 2 | 3 | 4 | 5 | 6 | 7 | 8 | 9 | 10 | 11 | 12 | 13 |

See **BODY STYLES** page 108

ELECTROMATIC JET SPARKLE

F/HOLE 2000-2003 *Electromatic across headstock, one f-hole.*
Similar to ELECTROMATIC JET SPARKLE, except:
* Semi-solid body with one f-hole; black (2620), black sparkle front (2625), silver sparkle front (2626), blue sparkle front (2627), gold sparkle front (2628), red sparkle front (2629).
See also SYNCHROMATIC SPARKLE JET F/HOLE.

ELECTROMATIC JUNIOR JET first

version 2000-2003 *Electromatic across headstock, one single-coil pickup.*
Similar to ELECTROMATIC JET CLUB, except:
* Dot markers.
* Sunburst (2101).
* One single-coil pickup.
* Two controls (one volume, one tone).
* Single-saddle wrapover bridge/tailpiece.
See also SYNCHROMATIC JUNIOR JET.

ELECTROMATIC JUNIOR JET second

version 2004-current *Electromatic down headstock, one humbucker pickup.*
Similar to ELECTROMATIC JUNIOR JET first version, except:
* Electromatic down headstock.
* Sunburst (5210), black (5215).
* One humbucker pickup.

ELECTROMATIC JUNIOR JET II first

version 2000-2003 *Electromatic across headstock, dot markers, two humbucker pickups.*
Similar to ELECTROMATIC JET CLUB, except:
* Dot markers.
* Redburst (2305).
* Two controls (one volume, one tone) and one selector.

* Single-saddle wrapover bridge/tailpiece.
See also SYNCHROMATIC JET II.

ELECTROMATIC JUNIOR JET II

second version 2004-current *Electromatic down headstock, dot markers, two humbucker pickups.*
Similar to ELECTROMATIC JUNIOR JET II first version, except:
* Electromatic down headstock.
* Sunburst (5220), black (5225).

ELECTROMATIC PRO JET 2004-current *Electromatic down headstock, half-moon markers, two humbucker pickups.*
* Bound rosewood fingerboard, half-moon markers, 22 frets; truss-rod adjuster at headstock; Electromatic down headstock.
* Semi-solid bound body; black front (5235), silver sparkle front (5236), gold sparkle front (5238).
* Two humbucker pickups.
* Two controls (one volume, one tone) and one selector.
* Coloured plastic pickguard.
* Six-saddle bridge, separate G-hole flat tailpiece.
Also black front, separate vibrato tailpiece (5235T).
Also silver sparkle front, separate vibrato tailpiece (5236T).
Also gold sparkle front, separate vibrato tailpiece (5238T).

ELECTROMATIC SPECIAL JET 2004-current *Electromatic down headstock, half-moon markers, two single-coil pickups.*
* Bound rosewood fingerboard, half-moon markers, 22 frets; truss-rod adjuster at headstock; Electromatic down headstock.

* Solid unbound body; sunburst (5250), black (5255), dark red (5259).
* Two single-coil pickups.
* Two controls (one volume, one tone) and one selector.
* Coloured plastic pickguard.
* Single-saddle wrapover bridge/tailpiece.

SYNCHROMATIC ELLIOT EASTON
2002-2003
Similar to ELECTROMATIC ELLIOT EASTON, except:
* Synchromatic on headstock.
* Green body front (1570).

SYNCHROMATIC JET BARITONE
2002-2003
Similar to ELECTROMATIC JET BARITONE, except:
* Synchromatic on headstock.
* Black sparkle front (1255).

SYNCHROMATIC JET CLUB 2000-2003 *Synchromatic on headstock, block markers.*
Similar to ELECTROMATIC JET CLUB, except:
* Synchromatic on headstock.
* Sunburst (1413).

SYNCHROMATIC JET PRO 2000-2003 *Synchromatic on headstock, crown markers.*
Similar to ELECTROMATIC JET PRO, except:
* Synchromatic on headstock.
* Black (1511), silver sparkle front (1512), sunburst (1514).
Also with separate vibrato tailpiece (1554).

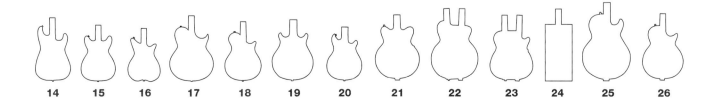

14   15   16   17   18   19   20   21   22   23   24   25   26

50 YEARS OF GRETSCH ELECTRICS

SYNCHROMATIC JET II 2000-2003
Synchromatic on headstock, dot markers, two humbucker pickups.
Similar to ELECTROMATIC JUNIOR JET II first version, except:
- Synchromatic on headstock.
- Redburst (1315).

SYNCHROMATIC JUNIOR JET 2000-2003
Similar to ELECTROMATIC JUNIOR JET first version, except:
- Synchromatic on headstock.
- Sunburst (1121), black (1122), red (1125), blue (1126), orange (1127), purple (1128).

SYNCHROMATIC SPARKLE JET
2000-current *Synchromatic on headstock, one humbucker pickup.*
Synchromatic on headstock, bound body.
Similar to ELECTROMATIC JET SPARKLE, except:
- Synchromatic on headstock.
- Black sparkle front (1615), silver sparkle front (1616), blue sparkle front (1617), gold sparkle front (1618), red sparkle front (1619).
Also black sparkle front, separate vibrato tailpiece (1615T).

SYNCHROMATIC SPARKLE JET F/HOLE 2000-current *Synchromatic on headstock, one f-hole.*
Similar to ELECTROMATIC JET SPARKLE F/HOLE, except:
- Synchromatic on headstock.
- Black sparkle front (1625), silver sparkle front (1626), blue sparkle front (1627), gold sparkle front (1628), red sparkle front (1629).
Also silver sparkle front, separate vibrato tailpiece (1626T).

STYLE FOUR (1957-60) USA
One sharp-pointed cutaway on small body

RAMBLER first version 1957-60 *One sharp-pointed cutaway and two large f-holes on small body.*
- Unbound rosewood fingerboard, dot markers; 20 frets; truss-rod adjuster at headstock.
- Hollow archtop bound body with two large f-holes; cream/black (6115).
- One single-coil pickup at neck.
- Two controls (volume, tone).
- Coloured plastic pickguard.
- Single-saddle wooden bridge, separate G-hole flat tailpiece.
Some examples in cream/green (6115). Succeeded by rounded-cutaway second version, see listing under STYLE FIVE.

STYLE FIVE (1960-62) USA
One rounded cutaway on small body

RAMBLER second version 1960-62 *One rounded cutaway and two large f-holes on small body.*
- Unbound rosewood fingerboard, dot markers; 20 frets; truss-rod adjuster at headstock.
- Hollow archtop bound body with two large f-holes; cream/black (6115).
- One single-coil pickup at neck.
- Two controls (volume, tone).
- Coloured plastic pickguard.
- Single-saddle wooden bridge, separate G-hole flat tailpiece.
Some examples in cream/green (6115). Succeeded sharp-pointed cutaway first version, see listing under STYLE FOUR.

STYLE FIVE (1998-current) Japan
One rounded cutaway on small body

ANNIVERSARY JUNIOR 6118JR 2002-current *Anniversary 1883-1993 on headstock.*
- Bound ebony fingerboard, half-moon markers, 22 frets; truss-rod adjuster at headstock; model nameplate on headstock.
- Hollow archtop bound body with two large f-holes; light/dark green (6118JR).
- Two humbucker pickups.
- Three controls (all volume) and two selectors.
- Coloured plastic pickguard.
- Six-saddle bridge, separate G-hole flat tailpiece.
Also ANNIVERSARY JUNIOR 6118TJR with separate vibrato tailpiece from c2004.

NASHVILLE JUNIOR 6120JR2 1996-current *Horseshoe on headstock, two large f-holes on small body, two humbuckers.*
- Bound ebony or rosewood fingerboard, half-moon markers, 22 frets; truss-rod adjuster at headstock.
- Hollow archtop bound body with two large f-holes; orange (6120JR2).
- Two humbucker pickups.
- Four controls (three volume, one tone) and one selector.
- Coloured plastic pickguard.
- Six-saddle bridge, separate vibrato tailpiece.
- Gold-plated hardware.
Also NASHVILLE JUNIOR 6120JR with one humbucker pickup 1996-98.

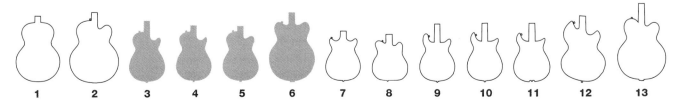

1   2   3   4   5   6   7   8   9   10   11   12   13

See **BODY STYLES** page 108

STYLE SIX (1961-81) USA

Twin shallow cutaways on large body

BLACK HAWK 1967-72 *Black Hawk on headstock.*

* Bound rosewood fingerboard, half-moon markers with dot markers from 15th fret; 22 frets plus zero fret; truss-rod adjuster at headstock; model nameplate on headstock.
* Hollow archtop bound body with two f-holes; sunburst (6100) c1967-70, or black (6101).
* Two humbucker pickups.
* Three controls (all volume) and three selectors.
* Coloured plastic pickguard.
* Bar-frame 'Floating Sound' unit plus six-saddle bridge, separate G-hole flat tailpiece.

BROADKASTER semi-hollow body first version 1975-77 *Dot markers, three controls and two selectors.*

* Unbound rosewood fingerboard, dot markers; 22 frets plus zero fret; truss-rod adjuster at headstock.
* Semi-hollow bound body with two f-holes; natural (7607) or sunburst (7608).
* Two humbucker pickups.
* Three controls (all volume) and two selectors.
* Coloured plastic pickguard.
* Six-saddle bridge/tailpiece.

Also in natural (7603) or sunburst (7604) with six-saddle bridge, separate vibrato tailpiece.

BROADKASTER semi-hollow body second version 1977-79 *Dot markers, five controls and one selector.*

Similar to first version, except:

* Red only (7609).
* Five controls (three volume, two tone) and one selector.

* Six-saddle wrapover bridge/tailpiece.

CHET ATKINS COUNTRY GENTLEMAN second version 1961-72 *Chet Atkins Country Gentleman on headstock, fake f-holes.*

* Bound ebony fingerboard, half-moon markers; 22 frets plus zero fret; truss-rod adjuster at headstock; model nameplate on headstock.
* Hollow archtop bound body with two fake f-holes; dark brown (6122).
* Two humbucker pickups.
* Three controls (all volume) and three selectors, plus one or two string damper controls.
* Coloured plastic pickguard (with model name from c1967).
* Single-saddle bridge, separate vibrato tailpiece.
* Gold-plated hardware.
* Pad on body back.
* Double string damper and two controls (single string damper and one control from c1966).

Some examples in black from c1967. Succeeded single-cutaway first version, see listing under STYLE TWO.

CHET ATKINS COUNTRY GENTLEMAN third version 1972-81

Chet Atkins Country Gentleman on pickguard, f-holes.

Similar to second version, except:

* Truss-rod adjuster at neck heel; no model nameplate on headstock.
* Hollow archtop body with two f-holes; brown (7670).
* Three controls (all volume) and two selectors from c1978.
* Six-saddle bridge.
* No pad on body back.
* No string damper and control.

Known as COUNTRY SQUIRE (7676) from c1981.

CHET ATKINS HOLLOW BODY 6120 second version 1961-64 *Chet Atkins logo on pickguard, fake f-holes, orange.*

* Bound ebony fingerboard, half-moon markers; 22 frets plus zero fret; truss-rod adjuster at headstock; horseshoe on headstock.
* Hollow archtop bound body with two fake f-holes; orange (6120).
* Two humbucker pickups.
* Three controls (all volume) and three selectors, plus one string damper control.
* Coloured plastic pickguard with Chet Atkins name.
* Single-saddle bridge, separate vibrato tailpiece.
* Gold-plated hardware.
* Pad on body back.
* String damper and control.

Succeeded single-cutaway first version, see listing under STYLE TWO.
Known as CHET ATKINS NASHVILLE from c1964-72; see separate listing.

CHET ATKINS NASHVILLE 6120 first version 1964-72 *Chet Atkins Nashville on headstock and pickguard, fake f-holes.*

Similar to CHET ATKINS HOLLOW BODY second version, except:

* Model nameplate on headstock.
* Model name on pickguard.

Previously known as CHET ATKINS HOLLOW BODY second version; see separate listing.

CHET ATKINS NASHVILLE 6120 second version 1972-80 *Chet Atkins Nashville on pickguard only, f-holes.*

Similar to CHET ATKINS HOLLOW BODY second version, except:

* Truss-rod adjuster at neck heel; no horseshoe or model nameplate on headstock.

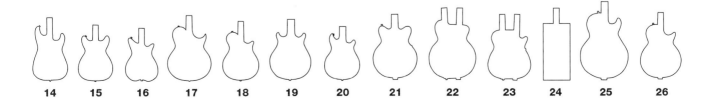

14   15   16   17   18   19   20   21   22   23   24   25   26

- Hollow archtop bound body with two f-holes; red (7660).
- Three controls (all volume) and two selectors from c1978.
- Coloured plastic pickguard with model name.
- Six-saddle bridge.
- No pad on body back.
- No string damper and control.

COUNTRY GENTLEMAN See CHET ATKINS COUNTRY GENTLEMAN listings.

COUNTRY SQUIRE See CHET ATKINS COUNTRY GENTLEMAN third version listing.

HOLLOW BODY See CHET ATKINS HOLLOW BODY second version listing.

MONKEES 1966-1969 *Monkees on truss-rod cover and pickguard.*
- Bound rosewood fingerboard, left and right half-moon markers; 22 frets plus zero fret; truss-rod adjuster at headstock; model nameplate on headstock; Monkees logo on truss-rod cover.
- Hollow archtop bound body with two f-holes; red (6123).
- Two humbucker pickups.
- Three controls (all volume) and three selectors.
- Coloured plastic pickguard with Monkees logo.
- Single-saddle bridge, separate vibrato tailpiece.

NASHVILLE See CHET ATKINS NASHVILLE listings.

RALLY 1967-69 *Half-moon/dot markers, diagonal stripes on truss-rod cover and pickguard.*
- Bound rosewood fingerboard, half-moon markers with dot markers from 15th fret; 22 frets plus zero fret; truss-rod adjuster at headstock; diagonal stripes on truss-rod cover.
- Hollow archtop bound body with two f-holes; green (6104) or yellow/brown (6105).
- Two single-coil pickups.
- Four controls (three volume, treble boost) and three selectors; active circuit.
- Coloured plastic pickguard with diagonal stripes.
- Single-saddle bridge, separate vibrato tailpiece.
Some examples with six-saddle bridge.

RONNY LEE 1962-63 *Ronny Lee on headstock, large fake f-holes.*
- Bound rosewood fingerboard, left and right half-moon markers; 22 frets plus zero fret; truss-rod adjuster at headstock; model nameplate on headstock.
- Hollow archtop bound body with two large fake f-holes; sunburst or brown.
- Two single-coil pickups.
- Three controls (all volume) and three selectors.
- Coloured plastic pickguard.
- Six-saddle bridge, separate vibrato tailpiece.
Some examples with single-saddle bridge.

SAM GOODY 1967 *Sam Goody on headstock, G-shape soundholes.*
- Bound rosewood fingerboard, half-moon markers with dot markers from 15th fret; 22 frets plus zero fret; truss-rod adjuster at headstock; model nameplate on headstock.
- Hollow archtop bound body with two G-shape soundholes; sunburst.
- Two single-coil pickups.
- Three controls (all volume) and three selectors.
- Coloured plastic pickguard.

- Single-saddle bridge, separate vibrato tailpiece.

STREAMLINER second version 1968-72 *Streamliner on headstock.*
- Bound rosewood fingerboard, half-moon markers with dot markers from 15th fret; 22 frets plus zero fret; truss-rod adjuster at headstock; model nameplate on headstock.
- Hollow archtop bound body with two f-holes; sunburst (6102) or red (6103).
- Two humbucker pickups.
- Three controls (all volume) and three selectors.
- Coloured plastic pickguard.
- Six-saddle bridge, separate G-hole flat tailpiece.

STREAMLINER third version 1972-75 *Half-moon markers, truss-rod adjuster at neck heel, G-hole flat tailpiece.*
Similar to first version, except:
- Half-moon markers (all); truss-rod adjuster at neck heel; no model nameplate on headstock.
- Sunburst (7565) c1972-73, or red (7566).

VIKING first version 1964-72 *Viking on headstock and pickguard.*
- Bound ebony fingerboard, half-moon markers with offset dot markers from 15th fret; 21 frets plus zero fret; truss-rod adjuster at headstock; model nameplate on headstock.
- Hollow archtop bound body with two large f-holes; sunburst (6187), natural (6188) or green (6189).
- Two humbucker pickups.
- Three controls (all volume) and three selectors, plus one string damper control.
- Coloured plastic pickguard with model name.

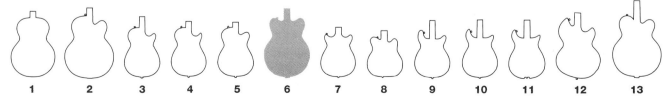

| 1 | 2 | 3 | 4 | 5 | 6 | 7 | 8 | 9 | 10 | 11 | 12 | 13 |

See **BODY STYLES** page 108

- Six-saddle bridge (bar-frame 'Floating Sound' unit plus six-saddle bridge from c1966), separate vibrato tailpiece.
- Gold-plated hardware.
- Pad on body back.
- String damper and control.

Some early examples with Viking ship logo and model name on pickguard.

VIKING second version 1972-75

Viking on pickguard only, truss-rod adjuster at neck heel.

Similar to first version, except:

- Truss-rod adjuster at neck heel; no model nameplate on headstock.
- Hollow archtop body with two f-holes; sunburst (7585) or natural (7586).
- Six-saddle bridge from c197?
- No pad on body back.
- No string damper and control.

WHITE FALCON second version

1962-72 White Falcon on headstock, falcon logo on pickguard.

- Bound ebony fingerboard, half-moon markers (with offset dot markers from 15th fret from c1964); 21 frets plus zero fret; truss-rod adjuster at headstock; model nameplate on headstock.
- Hollow archtop bound body with two large f-holes; white (6136).
- Two humbucker pickups.
- Three controls (all volume) and three selectors, plus two string damper controls.
- Coloured plastic pickguard with falcon logo.
- Six-saddle bridge (bar-frame 'Floating Sound' unit plus six-saddle bridge from c1966), separate G-logo tubular frame tailpiece (separate vibrato tailpiece from c1964).
- Gold-plated hardware.
- Pad on body back.

- Double string damper and two controls.

Some examples with three controls (all volume) and two selectors.
Vibrato tailpiece option c1962-64.
Succeeded single-cutaway first version, see listing under STYLE TWO.

WHITE FALCON third version 1972-

80 *Falcon logo on pickguard, truss-rod adjuster at neck heel.*

Similar to second version, except:

- Block position markers from c1974; truss-rod adjuster at neck heel; no model nameplate on headstock.
- Hollow archtop bound body with two f-holes; white (7594).
- Three controls (all volume) and two selectors from c1978.
- Six-saddle bridge from c1974.
- No double string damper and two controls from c1974.

Some examples with two large f-holes.

WHITE FALCON STEREO third

version 1962-72 *White Falcon on headstock, falcon logo on pickguard, two controls and five or six selectors.*

- Bound ebony fingerboard, half-moon markers (with offset dot markers from 15th fret from c1964); 21 frets plus zero fret; truss-rod adjuster at headstock; model nameplate on headstock.
- Hollow archtop bound body with two large f-holes; white (6137).
- Two humbucker pickups.
- Two controls (both volume) and six selectors (two controls – both volume – and five selectors, all on right body front, from c1965; two controls – both volume – and six selectors, including one on lower left body front, from c1966), plus two string damper controls.

- Coloured plastic pickguard with falcon logo.
- Six-saddle bridge (bar-frame 'Floating Sound' unit plus six-saddle bridge from c1966), separate G-logo tubular frame tailpiece (separate vibrato tailpiece from c1964).
- Gold-plated hardware.
- Pad on body back.
- Double string damper and two controls.

Vibrato tailpiece option c1962-64.
Some examples with two controls (both volume) and five selectors, plus two string damper controls c1962-65.
Succeeded single-cutaway second version, see listing under STYLE TWO.

WHITE FALCON STEREO fourth

version 1972-81 *Falcon logo on pickguard, truss-rod adjuster at neck heel, two controls and five or six selectors.*

Similar to WHITE FALCON STEREO third version, except:

- Block position markers from c1974; truss-rod adjuster at neck heel; no model nameplate on headstock.
- Hollow archtop bound body with two f-holes; white (7595).
- Two controls (both volume) and six selectors (two controls – both volume – and five selectors from c1978), plus two string damper controls c1972-74.
- Six-saddle bridge from c1974.
- No double string damper and two controls from c1974.

Some examples with two large f-holes.

12-STRING 1966-70 *Triangular markers, 12-string headstock.*

- Bound rosewood or ebony fingerboard, triangle markers; 22 frets plus zero fret; truss-rod adjuster at headstock; 12-string headstock.

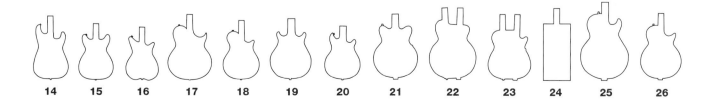

| 14 | 15 | 16 | 17 | 18 | 19 | 20 | 21 | 22 | 23 | 24 | 25 | 26 |

- Hollow archtop bound body with two large f-holes; sunburst (6075) or natural (6076).
- Two humbucker pickups.
- Three controls (all volume) and three selectors.
- Coloured plastic pickguard.
- Single-saddle wooden bridge, separate G-hole flat tailpiece.

Some examples with pad on body back. Some examples with string damper and control.

STYLE SIX (1989-current) Japan

Twin shallow cutaways on large body

BLACK FALCON 7594BK 1992-98

Falcon logo on pickguard, 22 frets, black.
Similar to WHITE FALCON 7594, except:
- Black (7594BK).

COUNTRY CLASSIC SPECIAL

G6122SP 2004-current *Model nameplate on headstock.*
Similar to COUNTRY CLASSIC 6122-1962, except:
- Single-saddle bridge.
- Pad on body back.
- Double string damper and two controls.

COUNTRY CLASSIC II 6122 1989-

current *Country Classic II on headstock and pickguard, f-holes.*
- Bound ebony fingerboard, half-moon markers; 22 frets; truss-rod adjuster at headstock; model nameplate on headstock.
- Hollow archtop bound body with two f-holes; dark brown (6122).
- Two humbucker pickups.
- Four controls (three volume, one tone) and one selector (three controls, all volume, and two selectors from c2003).

- Coloured plastic pickguard with model name.
- Six-saddle bridge, separate vibrato tailpiece.
- Gold-plated hardware.

COUNTRY CLASSIC 6122-12 12-string 1996-2001 *12-string headstock.*
Similar to COUNTRY CLASSIC 6122, except:
- 12-string headstock.
- Natural.
- Three controls (all volume) and three selectors.
- Separate G-hole flat tailpiece.

COUNTRY CLASSIC II 6122-1962

1993-current *Country Classic II on headstock and pickguard, fake f-holes, zero fret.*
Similar to COUNTRY CLASSIC 6122, except:
- 22 frets plus zero fret.
- Hollow archtop bound body with two fake f-holes.
- Three controls (all volume) and three selectors.
- Single-saddle bridge.

NASHVILLE DOUBLE CUTAWAY

6120DC 2003-current *Horseshoe on headstock, orange body.*
- Bound ebony fingerboard, half-moon markers, 22 frets; truss-rod adjuster at headstock; horseshoe on headstock.
- Hollow archtop bound body with two fake f-holes; orange (6120DC).
- Two humbucker pickups.
- Three controls (all volume) and three selectors, plus string damper control.
- Coloured plastic pickguard.
- Single-saddle bridge, separate vibrato tailpiece.
- Gold-plated hardware (except vibrato tailpiece).

- Pad on body back.
- String damper and control.

SILVER FALCON 7594SL 1995-98

Falcon logo on pickguard, 22 frets, black, chrome-plated hardware.
Similar to WHITE FALCON 7594, except:
- Black (7594SL).
- Chrome-plated hardware.

WHITE FALCON 7594 1989-current

Falcon logo on pickguard, 22 frets, white.
- Bound ebony fingerboard, block markers; 22 frets; truss-rod adjuster at headstock.
- Hollow archtop bound body with two f-holes; white (7594).
- Two humbucker pickups.
- Four controls (three volume, one tone) and one selector (three controls, all volume, and two selectors from c2003).
- Coloured plastic pickguard with falcon logo.
- Six-saddle bridge, separate vibrato tailpiece.
- Gold-plated hardware.

STYLE SEVEN (1961-70) USA

Twin semi-pointed cutaways on small body

CHET ATKINS SOLID BODY second

version 1961-62 *Orange body front, Chet Atkins logo on pickguard.*
- Bound ebony fingerboard, half-moon markers; 22 frets plus zero fret; truss-rod adjuster at headstock; horseshoe on headstock.
- Semi-solid bound body; orange front (6121).
- Two humbucker pickups.
- Three controls (all volume) and two selectors (three controls – all volume –

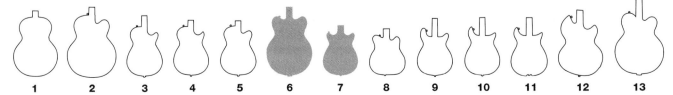

1   2   3   4   5   6   7   8   9   10   11   12   13

See **BODY STYLES** page 108

and three selectors from c1962).
• Coloured plastic pickguard with Chet Atkins logo.
• Single-saddle bridge, separate vibrato tailpiece.
• Gold-plated hardware.
Succeeded single-cutaway first version, see listing under STYLE THREE.

DUO JET second version 1961-70
Black body front.
• Bound rosewood fingerboard, half-moon markers; 22 frets plus zero fret; truss-rod adjuster at headstock.
• Semi-solid bound body; black front (6128).
• Two humbucker pickups.
• Three controls (all volume) and two selectors (three controls – all volume – and three selectors from c1962; four controls – three volume, treble boost – and three selectors from c1968).
• Coloured plastic pickguard.
• Six-saddle bridge, separate vibrato tailpiece.
• Gold-plated hardware from c1962.
Some examples with G-hole flat tailpiece. Also with various colour sparkle body fronts from c1963, previously known as SILVER JET second version, see separate listing.
Succeeded single-cutaway first version, see listing under STYLE THREE.

JET FIRE BIRD second version 1961-70
Red body front.
Similar to DUO JET second version, except:
• Black with red body front (6131).
Some examples with 21 frets.
Succeeded single-cutaway first version, see listing under STYLE THREE.

SILVER JET second version 1961-63
Silver sparkle body front.

Similar to DUO JET second version, except:
• Silver sparkle body front (6129).
Also other colour sparkle body front options from c1962.
Known as DUO JET second version with various colour sparkle body fronts from c1963, see separate listing.
Succeeded single-cutaway first version, see listing under STYLE THREE.

WHITE PENGUIN second version
1961-62 *White.*
• Bound ebony fingerboard, half-moon markers; 22 frets plus zero fret; truss-rod adjuster at headstock.
• Semi-solid bound body; white (6134).
• Two humbucker pickups.
• Three controls (all volume) and two selectors (three controls – all volume – and three selectors from c1962).
• Coloured plastic pickguard with penguin logo.
• Six-saddle bridge, separate vibrato tailpiece.
• Gold-plated hardware.
Some examples without penguin logo on pickguard.
Succeeded single-cutaway first version, see listing under STYLE THREE.

STYLE SEVEN (1996-current)
Japan
Twin semi-pointed cutaways on small body

DUO JET 6128T-1962 2001-current *Twin cutaways, black body front.*
• Bound rosewood fingerboard, half-moon markers, 22 frets; truss-rod adjuster at headstock.
• Semi-solid bound body; black front (6128T-62).
• Two humbucker pickups.

• Three controls (all volume) and two selectors.
• Coloured plastic pickguard.
• Six-saddle bridge, separate vibrato tailpiece.

MALCOLM YOUNG I 6131SMY 1996-current *Malcolm Young signature on truss-rod cover, one humbucker pickup, no pickguard, natural finish.*
• Bound ebony or rosewood fingerboard, half-moon markers, 22 frets; truss-rod adjuster at headstock; Malcolm Young signature on truss-rod cover.
• Semi-solid bound body; natural front (6131SMY), red front (6131SMYR), flame maple front (6131SMYF).
• One humbucker pickup.
• Two controls (one volume, one tone).
• Six-saddle wrapover bridge/tailpiece.

MALCOLM YOUNG II 6131MY 1996-current *Malcolm Young signature on truss-rod cover, two humbucker pickups, no pickguard, natural finish.*
Similar to MALCOLM YOUNG 6131SMY, except:
• Natural body front (6131MY), red body front (6131MYR), flame maple body front (6131MYF).
• Two humbucker pickups.
• Three controls (all volume) and two selectors.

SILVER JET 6129T-1962 1996-current
Twin cutaways, silver sparkle body front.
Similar to DUO JET 6128T-1962, except:
• Silver Sparkle body front.

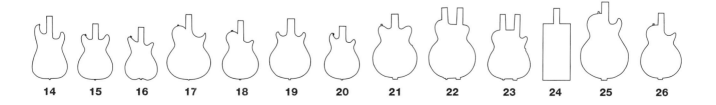

14   15   16   17   18   19   20   21   22   23   24   25   26

STYLE SEVEN (2000-current) Korea

Twin semi-pointed cutaways on small body

ELECTROMATIC DOUBLE JET first

version 2000-2003 *Electromatic across headstock, bolt-on neck.*

- Bolt-on neck with unbound rosewood fingerboard, dot markers, 22 frets; truss-rod adjuster at headstock; Gretsch on truss-rod cover; Electromatic across headstock.
- Semi-solid body; natural front (2910), black front (2921), silver sparkle front (2922), red front (2923).
- Two humbucker pickups.
- Three controls (all volume) and two selectors.
- Gretsch on coloured plastic pickguard.
- Six-saddle wrapover bridge/tailpiece.

Also silver sparkle front, separate vibrato tailpiece (2922T).

Some examples with Electromatic by Gretsch across headstock.

ELECTROMATIC DOUBLE JET

second version 2004-current *Electromatic down headstock, glued-in neck.*

- Bound rosewood fingerboard, half-moon markers, 22 frets; truss-rod adjuster at headstock; Electromatic down headstock.
- Semi-solid body; black front (5245T), silver sparkle front (5246T), gold sparkle front (5248T).
- Two humbucker pickups.
- Two controls (one volume, one tone) and one selector.
- Coloured plastic pickguard.
- Six-saddle bridge, separate vibrato tailpiece.

SYNCHROMATIC DOUBLE JET 2000-2003 *Synchromatic on headstock, twin cutaways.*

Similar to Electromatic Double Jet, except:

- Synchromatic on headstock.
- Natural front (1910), black front (1921), silver sparkle front (1922), red front (1923).

Also silver sparkle front, separate vibrato tailpiece (1922T).

STYLE EIGHT (1961-62) USA

Slightly-offset rounded cutaways on small body

BIKINI 1961-62 *Solid body with detachable slide-on hinged back section.*

- Unbound maple fingerboard, dot markers; 22 frets; truss-rod adjuster at body.
- Solid rectangular body centre section with detachable slide-on hinged back; black (6023).
- One single-coil pickup.
- Two controls (volume, tone), mounted on edge of body centre section.
- Wooden single-saddle bridge, separate trapeze tailpiece.

Some examples with zero fret.

Some examples with model name on headstock.

Some examples with coloured plastic pickguard.

Also guitar/bass double-neck (6025).

STYLE NINE (1961-62) USA

Two rounded cutaways (with longer left horn) on small body

CORVETTE solidbody first version 1961-62 *Slab body, one pickup.*

- Unbound rosewood fingerboard,

dot markers; 21 frets; truss-rod adjuster at body.

- Solid slab unbound body; dark brown (6132) or grey (6133).
- One single-coil pickup at bridge.
- Two controls (volume, tone) on pickguard.
- Coloured plastic pickguard.
- Wooden single-saddle bridge, separate trapeze tailpiece.

Succeeded by solidbody second version, see listing under STYLE TEN.

STYLE TEN (1962-64) USA

Two pointed cutaways (with long left horn) on small body

CORVETTE solidbody second

version one-pickup 1962-64 *Bevelled-edge body, one pickup.*

- Unbound rosewood fingerboard, dot markers; 21 frets; truss-rod adjuster at body (truss-rod adjuster at headstock from c1962).
- Solid bevelled-edge unbound body; dark red.
- One single-coil pickup at bridge.
- Two controls (volume, tone) on pickguard.
- Coloured plastic pickguard.
- Single-saddle bridge, separate trapeze tailpiece (6132) or separate vibrato tailpiece (6134).

Succeeded solidbody first version, see listing under STYLE NINE.

Succeeded by solidbody third version, see listing under STYLE ELEVEN.

CORVETTE solidbody second

version two-pickup 1963-64 *Bevelled-edge body, two pickups.*

Similar to CORVETTE solidbody first version one-pickup, except:

- Two single-coil pickups.

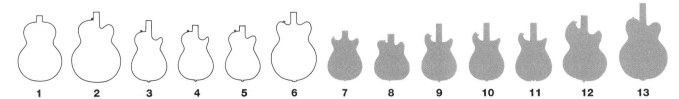

1   2   3   4   5   6   7   8   9   10   11   12   13

See **BODY STYLES** page 108

- Three controls (two volume, one tone) and three-way selector, all on pickguard.
- Single-saddle bridge, separate vibrato tailpiece (6135).

Succeeded by solidbody third version, see listing under STYLE ELEVEN.

PRINCESS 1962-63 *Bevelled-edge body, one pickup, pad on body back.*
Similar to CORVETTE solidbody second version one-pickup, except:
- Blue, pink or white (all 6106).
- Coloured plastic pickguard with model name.
- Single-saddle bridge, separate trapeze tailpiece.
- Gold-plated hardware.
- Pad on body back.
- Clip-on vibrato lever.

Some examples with no model name on pickguard.

TWIST 1962-63 *Bevelled-edge body, one pickup, red/white striped pickguard.*
Similar to CORVETTE solidbody second version one-pickup, except:
- Truss-rod adjuster at body.
- Red.
- Coloured stripe plastic pickguard.
- Separate trapeze tailpiece and clip-on vibrato lever (6109) or separate vibrato tailpiece (6110).

Some examples in yellow.

STYLE ELEVEN (1964-70) USA
Two pointed cutaways (with long left horn) on small body with cut-out in base.

'BLACK PRINCE' See PRINCE

CORVETTE solidbody third version one-pickup 1964-68 *Two and four tuners-per-side headstock, one pickup.*
- Unbound rosewood fingerboard, dot markers; 21 frets; truss-rod adjuster at headstock; two and four tuners-per-side headstock.
- Solid bevelled-edge body; red sunburst.
- One single-coil pickup.
- Two controls (volume, tone) on pickguard.
- Coloured plastic pickguard.
- Single-saddle bridge, separate trapeze tailpiece (6132) or separate vibrato tailpiece (6134).

Succeeded solidbody second version, see listing under STYLE TEN.

CORVETTE solidbody third version two-pickup 1964-70 *Two and four tuners-per-side headstock, two pickups.*
Similar to CORVETTE solidbody third version one-pickup, except:
- Two single-coil pickups.
- Three controls (two volume, one tone) and one selector (three controls – two volume, one tone – and two selectors from c1968), all on pickguard.
- Single-saddle bridge, separate vibrato tailpiece (6135).

Some examples in gold or silver metallic finish.
Succeeded solidbody second version, see listing under STYLE TEN.

'GOLD DUKE' See CORVETTE solidbody third version two-pickup listing.

PRINCE 1968-70 *Two and four tuners-per-side headstock, black, gold hardware*
Similar to CORVETTE solidbody third version two-pickup, except:
- Bound ebony fingerboard, half-moon markers.

- Black (6141).
- Two humbucker pickups.
- Gold-plated hardware.

Also known as 'BLACK PRINCE'.

'SILVER DUKE' See CORVETTE solidbody third version two-pickup listing.

STYLE TWELVE (1963-67) USA
Offset pointed cutaways on asymmetrically curved large body

ASTRO-JET 1963-67 *Astro-Jet on red/black body, four and two tuners-per-side headstock.*
- Bound ebony fingerboard, half-moon markers; 22 frets plus zero fret; truss-rod adjuster at headstock; four and two tuners-per-side headstock.
- Solid bevelled-edge unbound body with model nameplate on front; red/black (6126).
- Two humbucker pickups.
- Three controls (all volume) and three selectors, all on pickguard.
- Coloured plastic pickguard.
- Six-saddle bridge, separate vibrato tailpiece.

Some examples with 21 frets.
Some examples with single-saddle bridge.
Some examples with 'string tension' bar.

STYLE THIRTEEN (1972-80) USA
One rounded cutaway (and angled-in left upper bout) on large body

DELUXE CHET 1972-73 *Chet Atkins on pickguard, controls on body.*
- Bound ebony fingerboard, half-moon markers; 22 frets plus zero fret; truss-rod adjuster at neck heel.

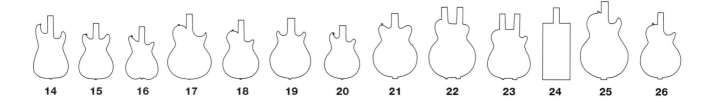

- Hollow archtop bound body with two f-holes; dark red (7680) or dark brown (7681).
- Two humbucker pickups.
- Five controls (three volume, two tone) and one selector.
- Coloured plastic pickguard with Chet Atkins name.
- Six-saddle bridge, separate vibrato tailpiece.
- Gold-plated hardware.

SUPER CHET 1972-80 *Super Chet on pickguard with controls along edge.*

- Bound ebony fingerboard, floral-style markers; 22 frets plus zero fret; truss-rod adjuster at neck heel; floral-style inlay on headstock.
- Hollow archtop bound body with two f-holes; dark red (7690) or dark brown (7691).
- Two humbucker pickups.
- Five controls (three volume, two tone) all mounted along edge of pickguard and one selector.
- Coloured plastic pickguard with name.
- Six-saddle bridge, separate frame-type tailpiece with floral-style insert (separate vibrato tailpiece option from c1977).
- Gold-plated hardware.

STYLE THIRTEEN (1998-2002) Japan

One rounded cutaway (and angled-in left upper bout) on large body

SUPER GRETSCH 7690 1998-2002 *Floral-style position markers and inlay on headstock.*

- Bound ebony fingerboard, floral-style markers, 22 frets; truss-rod adjuster at headstock; floral-style inlay on headstock.

- Hollow archtop bound body with two f-holes; sunburst (7690).
- Two humbucker pickups.
- Four controls (three volume, one tone) and one selector.
- Coloured plastic pickguard.
- Six-saddle bridge, separate vibrato tailpiece.
- Gold-plated hardware.

STYLE FOURTEEN (1975-77) USA

Offset rounded cutaways on small body

BROADKASTER solidbody version

1975-77 *Two pickups, all controls and jack socket on pickguard.*

- Bolt-on neck with unbound maple fingerboard, dot markers; 22 frets; truss-rod adjuster at headstock.
- Solid contoured unbound body; natural (7600) or sunburst (7601).
- Two humbucker pickups.
- Two controls (both volume), two selectors and jack socket, all on pickguard.
- Coloured plastic pickguard.
- Six-saddle bridge/tailpiece.

STYLE FIFTEEN (1977-81) USA

Twin rounded cutaways on small body

COMMITTEE 1977-81 *22-fret laminated through-neck.*

- Laminated through-neck with bound rosewood fingerboard, dot markers; 22 frets; truss-rod adjuster at neck heel.
- Solid contoured unbound body; brown (7628).
- Two humbucker pickups.
- Four controls (two volume, two tone) and one selector.
- Clear plastic pickguard.

- Six-saddle bridge/tailpiece with through-body stringing.
Some examples with coloured plastic pickguard.

STYLE SIXTEEN (1977-81) USA

Offset semi-pointed cutaways on small body with curved cut-out in base

TK 300 1977-81 *Six tuners-in-line headstock.*

- Bolt-on neck with unbound rosewood fingerboard, dot markers; 22 frets; truss-rod adjuster at neck heel; six tuners-in-line headstock with long Gretsch logo.
- Solid unbound body; red (7624) or natural (7625).
- Two humbucker pickups.
- Two controls (volume, tone) and one selector, all on pickguard.
- Coloured plastic pickguard.
- Six-saddle wrapover bridge/tailpiece.

STYLE SEVENTEEN (1977-80) USA

One sharp-pointed cutaway (and angled-in left upper bout) on large body

ATKINS AXE 1977-80 *Small block markers, controls on body.*

- Bound ebony fingerboard, small position markers; 22 frets plus zero fret; truss-rod adjuster at neck heel.
- Solid bound body; dark grey (7685) or red (7686).
- Two humbucker pickups.
- Four controls (two volume, two tone) and one selector.
- Coloured plastic pickguard.
- Six-saddle wrapover bridge/tailpiece.

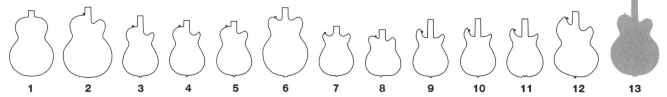

1   2   3   4   5   6   7   8   9   10   11   12   13

See **BODY STYLES** page 108

SUPER AXE 1977-80 *Small block markers, controls on elliptical plate.*
- Bound ebony fingerboard, small block markers; 22 frets plus zero fret; truss-rod adjuster at neck heel.
- Solid bound body; red (7680), dark grey (7681) or sunburst (7682).
- Two humbucker pickups.
- Five controls (volume, tone, sustain, phaser blend, phaser rate), two selectors and jack socket, all on elliptical plate; one selector on body; active circuit.
- Coloured plastic pickguard.
- Six-saddle wrapover bridge/tailpiece.

STYLE SEVENTEEN (1995-current) Japan

One sharp-pointed cutaway (and angled-in left upper bout) on large body

AXE 1995-2001 *Diced-type block markers, controls on body, truss-rod adjuster at headstock.*
- Bound rosewood fingerboard, dice-type block markers; 22 frets; truss-rod adjuster at headstock.
- Solid bound body; brown (7685), dark red (7686).
- Two humbucker pickups.
- Four controls (two volume, two tone) and one selector.
- Coloured plastic pickguard.
- Six-saddle wrapover bridge/tailpiece.

STYLE EIGHTEEN (1979-81) USA

One pointed cutaway (and angled-in left upper bout) on small body

BEAST BST-1000 one-pickup 1979-81 *24-fret bolt-on neck, one pickup.*
- Bolt-on neck with unbound rosewood

fingerboard, dot markers; 24 frets plus zero fret; truss-rod adjuster at headstock.
- Solid unbound body; brown (8210) or red (8216).
- One humbucker pickup.
- Two controls (volume, tone) and jack socket, all on pickguard.
- Coloured plastic pickguard.
- Six-saddle bridge/tailpiece with through-body stringing.
Also BEAST BST-1500 in brown (8217) from c1981.

BEAST BST-1000 two-pickup 1979-81 *24-fret bolt-on neck.*
Similar to BEAST BST-1000 one-pickup, except:
- Red (8211) or brown (8215).
- Two humbucker pickups.
- Two controls (volume, tone), one selector and jack socket, all on pickguard.

BEAST BST-1500 See BEAST BST-1000 listing.

STYLE NINETEEN (1979-80) USA

Twin pointed cutaways on small body

BEAST BST-2000 1979-80 *22-fret bolt-on neck.*
- Bolt-on neck with unbound rosewood fingerboard, dot markers; 22 frets plus zero fret; truss-rod adjuster at headstock.
- Solid unbound body; brown (8220) or red (8221).
- Two humbuckers.
- Two controls (volume, tone), one selector, one mini-switch and jack socket, all on pickguard.
- Coloured plastic pickguard.
- Six-saddle bridge/tailpiece with through-body stringing.

STYLE TWENTY (1979-81) USA

Offset pointed cutaways on small body

BEAST BST-5000 1979-81 *24-fret laminated through-neck, carved-edge body.*
- Laminated through-neck with bound rosewood fingerboard, dot markers; 24 frets plus zero fret; truss-rod adjuster at neck heel.
- Solid carved-edge unbound body; brown (8250).
- Two humbuckers.
- Four controls (two volume, two tone), one selector and one mini switch.
- Six-saddle bridge, separate bar tailpiece.

STYLE TWENTY-ONE (1997-current) Japan

Twin shallow cutaways on small body

COUNTRY CLASSIC JUNIOR 6122R 1998-current *Twin shallow cutaways and two large f-holes on small body.*
- Bound ebony or rosewood fingerboard, half-moon markers, 22 frets; truss-rod adjuster at headstock.
- Hollow archtop bound body with two large f-holes; dark brown, black.
- Two humbucker pickups.
- Four controls (three volume, one tone) and one selector.
- Coloured plastic pickguard.
- Six-saddle bridge, separate vibrato.
- Gold-plated hardware.
Also orange 2000-03.

WHITE FALCON JUNIOR 7594JR 1999-2002 *Twin shallow cutaways and two large f-holes on small white body, falcon logo on pickguard.*
- Bound ebony fingerboard, block

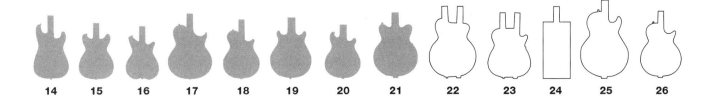

14   15   16   17   18   19   20   21   22   23   24   25   26

markers, 22 frets; truss-rod adjuster at headstock.
- Hollow archtop bound body with two large f-holes; white (7594JR).
- Two humbucker pickups.
- Four controls (three volume, one tone) and one selector.
- Coloured plastic pickguard with falcon logo.
- Six-saddle bridge, separate vibrato tailpiece.
- Gold-plated hardware.

STYLE TWENTY-TWO (1997-current) Japan

Two necks on one non-cutaway body

NASHVILLE 6120-6/12 double-neck
1997-current *12-string and 6-string necks on one non-cutaway body.*
- 12- and 6-string necks, each with bound ebony fingerboard, half-moon markers, 22 frets; truss-rod adjuster at headstock; horseshoe on headstock.
- Hollow archtop bound body with two f-holes; orange (6120-6/12).
- Two humbucker pickups per neck.
- Two controls (one volume, one tone) and two selectors.
- Six-saddle bridge per neck, separate G-hole flat tailpiece (12-string neck), separate vibrato tailpiece (6-string neck).
- Gold-plated hardware.

STYLE TWENTY-THREE (1998-current) Japan

Two necks on one single-cutaway body

DUO JET 6128T-6/12 double-neck
1998-current *12-string and 6-string necks on one single-cutaway body.*

- 12- and 6-string necks, each with bound ebony fingerboard, hump-top block markers, 22 frets; truss-rod adjuster at headstock; horseshoe on headstock.
- Semi-solid bound body; black (6128T-6/12).
- Two humbucker pickups per neck.
- Two controls (one volume, one tone) and two selectors.
- Six-saddle bridge per neck, separate G-hole flat tailpiece (12-string neck), separate vibrato tailpiece (6-string neck).

STYLE TWENTY-THREE (2004-current) Korea

Two necks on one single-cutaway body

ELECTROMATIC JET DOUBLE NECK
2004-current *Baritone and 6-string necks on one single-cutaway body.*
- Extended and standard scale length 6-string necks, each with bound rosewood fingerboard, dot markers, 22 frets; truss-rod adjuster at headstock; small Electromatic logo on headstock.
- Semi-solid bound body; silver sparkle front (5566).
- Two humbucker pickups per neck.
- Two controls (one volume, one tone) and three selectors.
- Six-saddle bridge per neck, separate vibrato tailpiece per neck.

SYNCHROMATIC SPARKLE JET DOUBLE-NECK 2002-03 *Baritone and 6-string necks on one single-cutaway body.*
Similar to ELECTROMATIC JET DOUBLE-NECK, except:
- Synchromatic on headstock.
- Silver sparkle front (1566).

STYLE TWENTY-FOUR (2000-current) Japan

Rectangular body

BO DIDDLEY 6138 2000-current *Rectangular body, Bo Diddley signature on truss-rod cover.*
- Unbound rosewood fingerboard, dot markers, 22 frets; truss-rod adjuster at headstock; Bo Diddley signature on truss-rod cover.
- Semi-solid bound body; red (6138).
- Two humbucker pickups.
- Four controls (three volume, one tone) and one selector.
- Six-saddle bridge, separate G-hole flat tailpiece.
- Gold-plated hardware.

STYLE TWENTY-FOUR (2000-current) Korea

Rectangular body

ELECTROMATIC BO DIDDLEY 2000-current *Rectangular body, Electromatic across headstock.*
- Bolt-on neck with unbound rosewood fingerboard, dot markers, 22 frets; truss-rod adjuster at headstock; Gretsch on truss-rod cover, Electromatic on headstock.
- Semi-solid body; red (2810, 5810).
- Two humbucker pickups.
- Four controls (three volume, one tone) and one selector.
- Six-saddle wrapover bridge/tailpiece.
Model number changed to 5810 from c2004.

SYNCHROMATIC BO DIDDLEY 2000-2003 *Rectangular body, Synchromatic on headstock.*
Similar to ELECTROMATIC BO DIDDLEY, except:

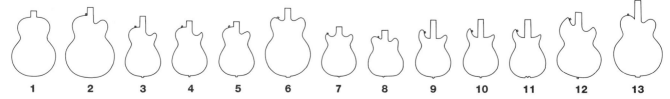

1   2   3   4   5   6   7   8   9   10   11   12   13

See **BODY STYLES** page 108

- Synchromatic on headstock.
- Red (1810).

STYLE TWENTY-FIVE (2002-03) Japan

One sharp-pointed cutaway on large body

NEW NASHVILLE 6120N 2002-2003
Single sharp-pointed cutaway on orange body.
- Bound rosewood fingerboard, hump-top block markers, 22 frets; truss-rod adjuster at headstock.
- Hollow archtop bound body with two large f-holes; orange (6120N).
- Two humbucker pickups.
- Four controls (three volume, one tone) and one selector.
- Coloured plastic pickguard.
- Six-saddle bridge, separate vibrato tailpiece.
- Gold-plated hardware.

STYLE TWENTY-SIX (2002-current) USA

One semi-pointed shallow cutaway on large body

SPECTRA SONIC LEAD 6143 2002-current *Spectra Sonic on truss-rod cover.*
- Unbound padouk fingerboard, dot markers, 22 frets; truss-rod adjuster at headstock; Spectra Sonic on truss-rod cover.
- Semi-solid unbound body; black (6143).
- Two humbucker pickups.
- Two controls (one volume, one tone) and one selector.
- White plastic pickguard.
- Six-saddle bridge, separate vibrato tailpiece.

SPECTRA SONIC C MELODY BARITONE 6144 2002-current *Spectra Sonic on truss-rod cover, extended scale length neck.*
Similar to SPECTRA SONIC LEAD, except:
- Extended scale length neck.

MISFITS, MAYBES, PROTOTYPES, POSSIBLES

As with other guitar makers, the Gretsch company was responsible for numerous one-offs, custom-built examples, evolving prototypes and special limited-production items (the latter often at the request of a dealer or individual customer). Many make frustratingly fleet appearances in Gretsch pricelists and literature with scant relevant information regarding specifications. The following is a list of the Gretsch guitars which seem to fit this 'could be' category. Some certainly existed in minimal numbers, and no doubt a few were made in at least small quantities, but others exist only in theory, usually as the result of some kind of misinformation.

BO DIDDLEY c1958-62
BO DIDDLEY CADILLAC c1961
BO DIDDLEY JUPITER c1961
BO DIDDLEY THUNDERBIRD c1961
CHET ATKINS JUNIOR c1970
CORVETTE (7623) c1976
CORVETTE II (7630) c1976-77
DELUXE CORVETTE (7632) c1976-77
HI ROLLER (7680) c1976
HI ROLLER (7685) c1978
ROC I (7635) c1976-77
SONGBIRD c1967-69
SOUTHERN BELLE (7176) c1983
STREAMLINER II (7667) c1973-75
SUPER ROC (7640) c1976-77
SUPER ROC II (7621) c1973-74

MISCELLANEOUS MAKES AND MODELS

Some guitars do not carry the Gretsch name prominently, but still have strong official connections with the company.

Japan
ELECTROMATIC by GRETSCH 1995-current
5120 Based on NASHVILLE 6120, see listing under STYLE TWO.
5122 Based on COUNTRY CLASSIC II 6122, see listing under STYLE SIX.
5128 Based on DUO JET 5128, see listing under STYLE THREE.
Cheaper equivalents made for Japanese domestic market only. Not to be confused with the Korean-made lines employing the same brandname, produced since 2000.

Korea
TW (TRAVELING WILBURYS) 1989-90
One rounded cutaway small slab body with travel-theme graphics on front.
TW-100 One single-coil pickup, three-saddle bridge/tailpiece.
TW-100T Similar to TW-100, except: six-saddle bridge/vibrato unit.
TW-200 Similar to TW-100, except: two single-coil pickups.
TW-300 One humbucker pickup, six-saddle bridge/vibrato unit.
TW-500 Two single-coil pickups, six-saddle bridge/tailpiece.
TW-600 Similar to TW-500, except: six-saddle bridge/vibrato unit.
Inexpensive solidbody models issued as a marketing tie-in with The Traveling Wilburys 'supergroup' and featuring the Wilbury-alias autographs of members Bob Dylan, George Harrison, Jeff Lynne, Roy Orbison and Tom Petty.

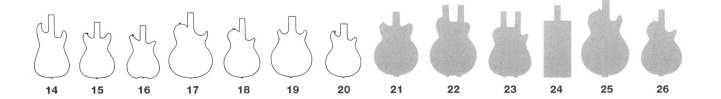

14   15   16   17   18   19   20   21   22   23   24   25   26

TERMINOLOGY & DATING

First we need to establish some terms used in the main listing, then find out how to date your Gretsch.

MODEL NAMES & NUMBERS
Some Gretsch models were given a number of different names at various times in company literature and pricelists. We've used the 'official' names throughout this reference section, as shown on the nameplate or logo on the instruments themselves or by consistent use in Gretsch printed material. Some models may be better known or equally well known by other names, and these have been noted and cross-referenced to the correct listing.

FRET COUNT
The number of frets can vary between examples of the same model. This has been noted in the listing where known, but additional variations may well exist.

PICKUPS
With Gretsch, the company's use of single-coil or humbucker pickups at various times gives a clue to the instrument's period of production, and these two broad pickup types have therefore been identified within each entry in the listing. Various designs of single-coil and humbucker pickups have been used by Gretsch over the years, but in the interests of clarity the differences have not been noted in the listing. In general on Gretsch guitars, a single-coil pickup can be identified by the presence of one row of six equally-spaced polepieces. Humbuckers, on the other hand, employ dual coils, usually indicated by two rows of six equidistant polepieces (though an exception is when

a plated metal cover is fitted that allows only one row of six polepieces to be visible, like the ones featured on models (for instance the TK300) from the mid to late 1970s.

COLOURED PLASTIC PICKGUARD
In typical fashion, Gretsch often made effective use of coloured plastic on their instruments, particularly for the pickguard, with gold and silver shades frequently replacing the more traditional black or tortoiseshell favoured by other makers. However, inconsistencies abound, making it extremely difficult to allocate colours to particular models at specific times, and so the definition 'coloured plastic pickguard' has been applied to all appropriate entries.

BRIDGES
Gretsch has employed a number of bridge designs over the years. In the interests of brevity these are not described in detail within the Reference Listing, but the various types include: Melita Synchrosonic (from about 1951), 'Bigsby bar' (from about 1955), Space Control (from about 1957), 'single metal bar' (from about 1957), Floating Sound (from about 1965), Adjustamatic (from about 1970), and Terminator (from about 1975), as well as a handful of single-saddle wooden varieties.

VIBRATO TAILPIECES
Many Gretsch guitars come with a separate vibrato tailpiece. Apart from a period during the early 1960s when a British-designed Burns unit was used on the solidbody models, Gretsch favoured the US Bigsby-made types. This was sometimes listed as an option for certain

models, although the Gretsch factory would fit a Bigsby to virtually any guitar if requested. The Bigsby vibrato tailpiece was equally easy to retro-fit and many Gretsches turn up with a Bigsby fitted by the owner after purchase. In view of all this, the presence of a separate vibrato tailpiece has only been noted when it was officially offered in Gretsch literature. Various different types of Bigsby units were used by Gretsch, but again in the interests of clarity these differences are not mentioned in the listing.

DATING GRETSCH ELECTRICS
Establishing the age of an instrument is an important necessity for most owners, especially those who possess vintage examples, because age has a direct relationship to value. Many Gretsch models from the 1950s and 1960s have long been elevated to collectable status, thanks as much to their image and associations with famous players as to inherent quality.

Gretsch guitars, like those from virtually every other manufacturer, are hard to date with unquestionable precision, and an approximate age should be regarded as a safe and satisfying compromise.

Serial numbers can offer an indication of the production period, if not always a specific year. Using serial numbers as the sole method of dating is not advisable: numbering systems tend to be inconsistent or incomplete and can include confusing duplication or repetition. Such vagaries afflict the serial number schemes employed by most guitar makers, and Gretsch is certainly no exception. Other clues should wherever possible be used to confirm the age of a Gretsch guitar.

GRETSCH SERIAL NUMBERS
1949-65 (USA)

Prior to 1949 Gretsch numbering was haphazard, with a series starting at 001 applied to only some of a predominantly acoustic range. In 1949 a new system began for most models and remained in use until 1965. Although on paper it appears straightforward, the numbers were not always applied in strict sequence or chronological order, and anachronistic anomalies can and do occur.

Number Series	Approx period
3000s	1949-50
4000s to 5000s	1951
5000s to 6000s	1952
6000s to 8000s	1953
9000s to 13,000s	1954
12,000s to 16,000s	1955
17,000s to 21,000s	1956
21,000s to 26,000s	1957
26,000s to 30,000s	1958
30,000s to 34,000s	1959
34,000s to 39,000s	1960
39,000s to 45,000s	1961
46,000s to 52,000s	1962
53,000s to 63,000s	1963
63,000s to 78,000s	1964
78,000s to 85,000s	1965

GRETSCH SERIAL NUMBERS
1965-72 (USA)

In 1965 the previous system was replaced by a new method that incorporated the date of manufacture. The number of digits used could vary from three to six: the first or first and second digit(s) indicate(s) production month (from *1* to *12*); the next digit denotes the last number of the relevant year (from 196*5* to 197*2*); and any remaining digits refer to the model itself.

For example:
592 suggests May (*5*) 1969 (*9*)
7820 suggests July (*7*) 1968 (*8*)
96220 suggests September (*9*) 1966 (*6*)
271376 suggests February (*2*) 1967 (*7*)

However, it should be noted that certain combinations can cause confusion about the date. Months 10, 11 and 12 (October, November and December respectively) could also indicate month 1 (January) and years 0, 1 and 2 (1970, 1971 and 1972 respectively). In these instances other dating pointers must be used to confirm the guitar's true age.

GRETSCH SERIAL NUMBERS
1972-81 (USA)

The previous numbering scheme continued in operation until 1981, but from about 1972 the month digits were frequently separated from the rest of the serial number by a hyphen, or a dot, or a space. This small difference helps to prevent any confusion about the year digit, which otherwise could often apply to both the 1965-72 and 1972-81 production periods. The visible presence of hyphen, dot or space within the number usually confirms that it relates to 1972-81.

For example:
3-8094 suggests March (*3*) 1978 (*8*)
5.5125 suggests May (*5*) 1975 (*5*)
4 2126 suggests April (*4*) 1972 (*2*)

GRETSCH SERIAL NUMBERS
1989-c2003 (Japan)

When Gretsch guitar production began again in 1989 a different sequence was used, consisting of six digits plus a three-digit suffix.

With typical Japanese logic, the first part provides the year of manufacture by the first two digits, while the fourth, fifth and sixth digits are part of the relevant model number.

For example:
901121-154 suggests 1990 (*90*), Round Up 6121 (*121*)
946119-982 suggests 1994 (*94*), Tennessee Rose 6119 (*119*)

GRETSCH SERIAL NUMBERS
c2003-current (Japan)

When Fender started to manufacture Gretsch guitars starting in 2003, the company used a number of its long-standing Japanese factory sources for many of the models, principally Terada. Fender-era serial numbers use a eight-digit serial number with a two-letter prefix. The first two letters indicate country of origin (usually J for Japan) and factory (often T for Terada). For the numbers, ignore the first one (usually a zero); the next two indicate the last two digits of the year, the following two the month, and the last four digits represent the number of the particular instrument among the total guitars built that year.

For example:
JT04075003 suggests July (*07*) 2004 (*04*)

OTHER DATING FEATURES

In addition to the serial number, a number of other features can be used to help in dating a Gretsch guitar – although the company, unlike some manufacturers, made comparatively few changes that affected the majority of the models in its line at any given time. Gretsch is renowned for a succession of gimmicky features that made their mark on various models at varied intervals, but some less specific aspects can still be regarded as dating landmarks, as follows, at least for some models.

POSITION MARKERS

At first Gretsch electrics featured types of fingerboard position markers that were already employed on their acoustic brethren: conventional dots or blocks, or the more distinctive and fancier 'hump-top' variation of blocks. While dots continued in use on cheaper Gretsches, the unique half-moon 'neo-classic' position markers were introduced to the remainder of the line in about 1957.

These were used until 1981, but block markers were revived for some models around 1974. Gretsch used other types too, but only on certain instruments, so these do not serve as general dating pointers. The current line features blocks, 'hump-top' blocks, and half-moon markers, used as appropriate to the original production period being suggested by each of the 'new' models.

ZERO FRET

This is a fret placed directly in front of the nut. It is used to determine string height, and so relegates the nut to a mere string guide. More commonly favoured on instruments of European origin, the zero fret (fancifully described in company literature as the 'Action-flow fret nut') appeared on many Gretsch models from around 1959, remaining in use until 1981. It is employed on the current lines, but only on the models related to old production periods.

TRUSS-ROD ADJUSTER

On the majority of Gretsch models the truss-rod adjuster was originally located on the headstock, under a cover, but from about 1972 it was moved to a location behind the neck heel, accessed through the back of the body. This was the visible indication of a new truss-rod system, introduced by Gretsch's new owners, Baldwin, and previously used on guitars made by Burns, a British company acquired by Baldwin in 1965 (Baldwin ceased production of Burns instruments in 1970). The Burns-designed 'gear-box'-controlled truss-rod then appeared on many Gretsch models until 1981.

MADE IN USA

Following the takeover of Gretsch by Baldwin in 1967, 'Made In USA' was stamped on the rear of the headstock, alongside the serial number. This continued until about 1973.

BODY

Gretsch followed Gibson's fashion by introducing twin-cutaway styling on various of the popular hollowbody and semi-solidbody models from about 1961. The semi-solids reverted to single-cutaway design around eight years later, again reflecting the popularity of Gibson designs.

Gretsch employed large f-holes on many of its hollowbody guitars until about 1972, but from then on the f-holes on these models became smaller and of more standard type. 'Fake' f-holes (blocked-in or painted-on f-holes) were a unique Gretsch feature introduced on certain models around 1957, but these were replaced by the real thing from about 1972.

PICKUPS

Around 1957 Gretsch introduced a humbucking pickup to replace the single-coil type made for them by DeArmond, which until then had been the type used on all Gretsch's electrics.

The new Filter'Tron pickup was featured on many models from then on, later being joined by other humbucker units such as the Super'Tron around 1963.

Conversely, in about 1960 Gretsch came up with its own single-coil pickup, the Hi-Lo'Tron, and this was then employed on various cheaper hollow body and solidbody instruments.

The current lines feature revised versions of the Filter'Tron humbucker and DeArmond-style single-coil pickups, and occasionally a Super'Tron, as appropriate to 'vintage'.

CONTROLS AND CIRCUITRY

Partnering the launch of the new Filter'Tron humbucker pickup came a revised circuitry system. Gretsch abandoned conventional rotary tone controls and instead fitted toggle-type selectors to provide 'preset' tone changes. From around 1970 the company returned to normal tone controls, but for some models only; others retained the tone selectors until 1981. The current lines employ both types of control layout, again relevant to the original production period being revived by each model.

Another date-related control was the standby switch, a unique Gretsch feature. This addition to many up-scale models, used from about 1961 to 1978, allowed the instrument to be turned off without disconnecting the lead. Again this is employed on the current models where appropriate.

PICKGUARD

From about 1970 a more angular, 'squared-off' style of pickguard replaced the original curvaceous Gretsch design, and is one of the very few changes made that is common to virtually all models.

CONTROL POT CODES

The metal casings of many US-made control potentiometers (usually called 'pots') are stamped with code numbers that can include date information, therefore providing useful confirmation of an instrument's age.

However, be aware that pots were not always used immediately, and also that they may have been replaced at some time – factors that could cause contradiction and confusion.

The code consists of six or seven numbers. Of these the first three identify the manufacturer and can be disregarded for our purposes, while the final two indicate the week of the production year and are also unimportant for our purposes.

In a six-digit code it is the fourth number that indicates the last digit of the appropriate year during the 1950s: 195?. In a seven-digit code, the fourth and fifth numbers signify the last two digits of any year thereafter.

MODEL NUMBERS & NAMES

Gretsch has given real names to virtually all its models. Many instruments carry the name on headstock and/or pickguard, which can provide easy identification – but please note that the company has sometimes used the same name for radically different instruments. Another useful ID clue is provided by the four-digit model number – not to be confused with the serial number – that is allocated to most models. This can usually be found on a label posted somewhere within the instrument.

Gretsch has given different numbers for variations in construction, components and (especially) cosmetics, so the code can be a helpful pointer to identity. However, there has been considerable repetition and duplication of numbers, and this can cause confusion, so further indicators should be used to confirm the precise model.

Look up the number here to discover the model name; go to the page number in the Reference listing for more info.

USA

Model No.	Model name	Page(s)
6023	Bikini	128
6025	Bikini	128
6075	12-string	125
6076	12-string	125
6079	Van Eps	112
6080	Van Eps	112
6081	Van Eps	112
6082	Van Eps	112
6100	Black Hawk	123
6101	Black Hawk	123
6101	Country Club Stereo	111
6102	Country Club Stereo	111
6102	Streamliner	124
6103	Country Club Stereo	111
6103	Streamliner	124
6104	Rally	124
6105	Rally	124
6106	Princess	129
6109	Twist	129
6110	Twist	129
6111	Anniversary Stereo	109
6112	Anniversary Stereo	109
6115	Rambler	122
6117	'Cat's Eye Custom'	109
6117	Anniversary	109
6118	Anniversary	109
6119	Chet Atkins Tennessean	110
6120	Chet Atkins Hollow Body 6120	109, 123
6120	Chet Atkins Nashville 6120	123
6120W-1955	Nashville 1955 Custom Western	112
6120WCST	Nashville Western 6120WCST	111
6120-1955	Nashville 1955 Custom	112
6121	Chet Atkins Solid Body	117, 126
6122	Chet Atkins Country Gentleman	109, 123
6123	Monkees	124
6124	Anniversary	108
6125	Anniversary	108
6126	Astro-Jet	129
6127	Roc Jet	118
6128	Duo Jet	118, 127

Model No.	Model name	Page(s)
6129	Silver Jet	118, 127
6130	Roc Jet	118
6130	Round Up	118
6131	Jet Fire Bird	118, 127
6132	Corvette	128, 129
6133	Corvette	128
6134	Corvette	128, 129
6134	White Penguin	119, 127
6135	Corvette	128, 129
6136	White Falcon	112, 125
6136CST	White Falcon 6136CST	113
6136-1955	White Falcon 1955 Custom	113
6137	White Falcon Stereo	113, 125
6141	Prince	129
6143	Spectra Sonic Lead	133
6144	Spectra Sonic C Melody Baritone	133
6182	Corvette	108
6182	Electromatic Spanish	108
6183	Corvette	108
6183	Electromatic Spanish	108
6184	Corvette	108
6185	Electromatic Spanish	108
6186	Clipper	108, 110
6187	Clipper	108, 110
6187	Electro II	108
6187	Viking	124
6188	Clipper	108
6188	Electro II	108
6188	Viking	124
6189	Electromatic	111
6189	Streamliner	112
6189	Viking	124
6190	Electromatic	111
6190	Streamliner	112
6191	Electromatic	111
6191	Streamliner	112
6192	Country Club	110
6192	Electro II	111
6193	Country Club	110
6193	Electro II	111
6196	Country Club	110
6196-1955	Country Club 1955 Custom	111
6199	Convertible	110

Model No.	Model name	Page
6199	Sal Salvador	112
7555	Clipper	110
7560	Anniversary	109
7565	Streamliner	124
7566	Streamliner	124
7575	Country Club	111
7576	Country Club	111
7577	Country Club	111
7580	Van Eps	112
7581	Van Eps	112
7585	Viking	125
7586	Viking	125
7593	White Falcon	113
7593	White Falcon Stereo	113
7594	White Falcon	125
7595	White Falcon Stereo	125
7600	Broadkaster	130
7601	Broadkaster	130
7603	Broadkaster	123
7604	Broadkaster	123
7607	Broadkaster	123
7608	Broadkaster	123
7609	Broadkaster	123
7610	Roc Jet	118
7611	Roc Jet	118
7612	Roc Jet	118
7613	Roc Jet	118
7620	Country Roc	118
7621	Roc II	118
7624	TK 300	130
7625	TK 300	130
7628	Committee	130
7655	Chet Atkins Tennessean	110
7660	Chet Atkins Nashville	123
7670	Chet Atkins Country Gentleman	123
7680	Deluxe Chet	129
7680	Super Axe	131
7681	Deluxe Chet	129
7681	Super Axe	131
7682	Super Axe	131
7685	Atkins Axe	130
7686	Atkins Axe	130
7690	Super Chet	130
7691	Super Chet	130
8210	Beast BST-1000	131
8211	Beast BST-1000	131
8215	Beast BST-1000	131
8216	Beast BST-1000	131
8217	Beast BST-1500	131
8220	Beast BST-2000	131
8221	Beast BST-2000	131
8250	Beast BST-5000	131

JAPAN

The more recent Japanese-made Gretsch electrics adopt a similar system of model numbers. Some of the original numbers have been used for the revived models or near-equivalents of old models.

Model No.	Model name	Page(s)
400CV	Synchromatic 400CV	116
400MCV	Synchromatic 400MCV	116
6022CV	Rancher 6022CV	116
6040MC-SS	Synchromatic 6040MC-SS	116
6114	New Jet	119
6117	Anniversary	113
6117HT	Anniversary	113
6117THT	Anniversary	113
6118	Anniversary	113
6118JR	Anniversary Junior 6118JR	122
6118T	Anniversary 6118T	113
6118T-120	Anniversary 6118T-120	114
6118TJR	Anniversary Junior 6118TJR	122
6119	Tennessee Rose 6119	116
6119SP	Tennessee Special 6119SP	116
6119-1962FT	Tennessee Rose 6119-1962FT	116
6119-1962HT	Tennessee Rose 6119-1962HT	116
6120	Nashville 6120	115
6120AM	Nashville 6120AM	115
6120BK	Nashville 6120BK	115
6120BS	Nashville 6120BS	115
6120DC	Nashville Double Cutaway 6120DC	126
6120DE	Duane Eddy 6120DE	114
6120DEO	Duane Eddy 6120DEO	114
6120DS	Nashville Dynasonic 6120DS	115
6120DSW	Nashville Dynasonic 6120DSW	115
6120GA	Nashville Golden Anniversary 6120GA	115
6120GR	Nashville 6120GR	115
6120JR	Nashville Junior 6120JR	122
6120JR2	Nashville Junior 6120JR2	122
6120KS	Nashville Keith Scott 6120KS	115
6120N	New Nashville	133
6120SH	Nashville Brian Setzer Hot Rod	115
6120SSL	Nashville Brian Setzer	115
6120SSLVO	Nashville Brian Setzer	115
6120SSU	Nashville Brian Setzer	115
6120SSUGR	Nashville Brian Setzer	115
6120TM	Nashville 6120TM	115
6120W	Nashville Western 6120W	115
6120W-1957	Nashville Western 6120W-1957	115
6120-1960	Nashville 6120-1960	115
6120-6/12	Nashville 6120-6/12 double neck	132
6121	Round Up 6121	119
6121W	Round Up 6121W	119
6122	Country Classic II 6122	126
6122R	Country Classic Junior 6122R	131
6122S	Country Classic I 6122S	114
6122SP	Country Classic Special 6122SP	126
6122-12	Country Classic 6122-12 12-string	126
6122-1958	Country Classic 6122-1958	114
6122-1959	Nashville Classic 6122-1959	115
6122-1962	Country Classic II 6122-1962	126
6124	Anniversary	114
6125	Anniversary	114
6128	Duo Jet 6128	119
6128-1957	Duo Jet 6128-1957	119
6128T-6/12	Duo Jet 6128T-6/12 double neck	132
6128T-1962	Duo Jet 6128T-1962	127
6128TBEE	Elliot Easton 6128TBEE	119
6128TEE	Elliot Easton 6128TEE	119
6128TREE	Elliot Easton 6128TREE	119
6128TSP	Duo Jet Special 6128TSP	119
6129	Silver Jet 6129	119

6129-1957	Silver Jet 6129-1957	120
6129-1957	Sparkle Jet 6129-1957	120
6129T	Sparkle Jet 6129T	120
6129T-1962	Silver Jet 6129T-1962	127
6131	Jet Firebird 6131	119
6131MY	Malcolm Young II	127
6131MYF	Malcolm Young II	127
6131MYR	Malcolm Young II	127
6131SMY	Malcolm Young I	127
6131SMYF	Malcolm Young I	127
6131SMYR	Malcolm Young I	127
6131T	Jet Firebird 6131T	119
6134	White Penguin	120
6134B	Black Penguin	119
6136	White Falcon 6136	116
6136BK	Black Falcon 6136BK	114
6136SL	Silver Falcon 6136SL	116
6136T	White Falcon 6136T	116
6136TBK	Black Falcon 6136TBK	114

6136TSL	Silver Falcon 6136TSL	116
6136-1958	White Falcon Stephen Stills 6136-1958	117
6138	Bo Diddley 6138	132
6192	Country Club	114
6192T	Country Club	114
6193	Country Club	114
6193T	Country Club	114
6196	Country Club 6196	114
6196T	Country Club 6196T	114
7593	White Falcon 7593	117
7593BK	Black Falcon 7593BK	114
7594	White Falcon 7594	126
7594BK	Black Falcon 7594BK	126
7594JR	White Falcon Junior 7594JR	131
7594SL	Silver Falcon 7594SL	126
7685	Axe	131
7686	Axe	131
7690	Super Gretsch	130

KOREA

Model No.	Model name	Page(s)
1121	Synchromatic Junior Jet	122
1122	Synchromatic Junior Jet	122
1125	Synchromatic Junior Jet	122
1126	Synchromatic Junior Jet	122
1127	Synchromatic Junior Jet	122
1128	Synchromatic Junior Jet	122
1255	Synchromatic Jet Baritone	121
1315	Synchromatic Jet II	122
1413	Synchromatic Jet Club	121
1511	Synchromatic Jet Pro	121
1512	Synchromatic Jet Pro	121
1514	Synchromatic Jet Pro	121
1554	Synchromatic Jet Pro	121
1566	Synchromatic Sparkle Jet Double-Neck	132
1570	Synchromatic Elliot Easton	121
1615	Synchromatic Sparkle Jet	122
1615T	Synchromatic Sparkle Jet	122
1616	Synchromatic Sparkle Jet	122
1617	Synchromatic Sparkle Jet	122
1618	Synchromatic Sparkle Jet	122
1619	Synchromatic Sparkle Jet	122
1625	Synchromatic Sparkle Jet F/Hole	122
1626	Synchromatic Sparkle Jet F/Hole	122
1626T	Synchromatic Sparkle Jet F/Hole	122
1627	Synchromatic Sparkle Jet F/Hole	122
1628	Synchromatic Sparkle Jet F/Hole	122
1629	Synchromatic Sparkle Jet F/Hole	122
1810	Synchromatic Bo Diddley	132
1910	Synchromatic Double Jet	128
1921	Synchromatic Double Jet	128
1922	Synchromatic Double Jet	128
1922T	Synchromatic Double Jet	128
1923	Synchromatic Double Jet	128
2101	Electromatic Junior Jet	121
2305	Electromatic Junior Jet II	121
2403	Electromatic Jet Club	120
2504	Electromatic Jet Pro	120
2554	Electromatic Jet Pro	120
2610	Electromatic Jet Sparkle	120

2615	Electromatic Jet Sparkle	120
2616	Electromatic Jet Sparkle	120
2617	Electromatic Jet Sparkle	120
2618	Electromatic Jet Sparkle	120
2619	Electromatic Jet Sparkle	120
2620	Electromatic Jet Sparkle F/Hole	121
2625	Electromatic Jet Sparkle F/Hole	121
2626	Electromatic Jet Sparkle F/Hole	121
2627	Electromatic Jet Sparkle F/Hole	121
2628	Electromatic Jet Sparkle F/Hole	121
2629	Electromatic Jet Sparkle F/Hole	121
2810	Electromatic Bo Diddley	132
2910	Electromatic Double Jet	128
2921	Electromatic Double Jet	128
2922	Electromatic Double Jet	128
2922T	Electromatic Double Jet	128
2923	Electromatic Double Jet	128
3110	Historic Series Synchromatic	117
3140	Historic Series Thinline Synchromatic	117
3141	Historic Series Thinline Synchromatic	117
3150	Historic Series Streamliner	117
3151	Historic Series Streamliner	117
3155	Historic Series Streamliner	117
3156	Historic Series Streamliner	117
3900	Historic Series Synchromatic Jr	117
3905	Historic Series Synchromatic Jr	117
3967	Historic Series Synchromatic Jr	117
5125	Electromatic Hollow Body	117
5126	Electromatic Hollow Body	117
5127	Electromatic Hollow Body	117
5128	Electromatic Hollow Body	117
5129	Electromatic Hollow Body	117
5210	Electromatic Junior Jet	121
5215	Electromatic Junior Jet	121
5220	Electromatic Junior Jet II	121
5225	Electromatic Junior Jet II	121
5235	Electromatic Pro Jet	121
5235T	Electromatic Pro Jet	121
5236	Electromatic Pro Jet	121
5236T	Electromatic Pro Jet	121
5238	Electromatic Pro Jet	121
5238T	Electromatic Pro Jet	121

5245T	Electromatic Double Jet	128
5246T	Electromatic Double Jet	128
5248T	Electromatic Double Jet	128
5250	Electromatic Special Jet	121
5255	Electromatic Special Jet	121

5259	Electromatic Special Jet	121
5265	Electromatic Jet Baritone	120
5566	Electromatic Jet Double Neck	132
5570	Electromatic Elliot Easton	120
5810	Electromatic Bo Diddley	132

MODEL CHRONOLOGY

MODELS AND YEARS

This listing here and opposite, split into the three centres of production, shows the electric models produced by Gretsch in chronological order of production.

USA

Electromatic Spanish 1st version	1939-42
Electromatic Spanish 2nd version	1949-54
Electro II 1st version	1951-54
Electro II 2nd version	1951-54
Electromatic	1951-54
Duo Jet 1st version	1953-62
Corvette hollow body version	1954-56
Country Club 1st, 2nd, 3rd & 4th versions	1954-81
Round Up	1954-59
Silver Jet 1st version	1954-61
Streamliner 1st version	1954-59
Chet Atkins Hollow Body 1st version	1955-61
Chet Atkins Solid Body 1st version	1955-61
Convertible	1955-69
Jet Fire Bird 1st version	1955-61
White Falcon 1st version	1955-62
White Penguin 1st version	1955-61
Clipper 1st version	1956-58
Chet Atkins Country Gentleman 1st version	1957-61
Clipper 2nd & 3rd versions	1957-75
Rambler 1st version	1957-60
Anniversary one-pickup	1958-72
Anniversary two-pickup 1st, 2nd & 3rd versions	1958-77
Chet Atkins Tennessean 1st, 2nd & 3rd versions	1958-80
Country Club Stereo 1st & 2nd versions	1958-65
White Falcon Stereo 1st & 2nd versions	1958-62
Sal Salvador	1959-67
Rambler 2nd version	1960-62
Anniversary Stereo	1961-63
Bikini	1961-62
Chet Atkins Country Gentleman 2nd & 3rd versions	1961-81
Chet Atkins Hollow Body 2nd version	1961-64
Chet Atkins Solid Body 2nd version	1961-62
Corvette solidbody 1st version	1961-62
Duo Jet 2nd version	1961-70
Jet Fire Bird 2nd version	1961-70
Silver Jet 2nd version	1961-63
White Penguin 2nd version	1961-62
Corvette solidbody 2nd version one-pickup	1962-64

Princess	1962-63
Ronny Lee	1962-63
Twist	1962-63
White Falcon 2nd & 3rd versions	1962-80
White Falcon Stereo 3rd & 4th versions	1962-81
Astro-Jet	1963-67
Corvette solidbody 2nd version two-pickup	1963-64
'Cat's-Eye Custom'	1964-67
Chet Atkins Nashville 1st & 2nd versions	1964-80
Corvette solidbody 3rd version one-pickup	1964-68
Corvette solidbody 3rd version two-pickup	1964-70
Viking 1st & 2nd versions	1964-75
Monkees	1966-69
12-string	1966-70
Black Hawk	1967-72
Rally	1967-69
Sam Goody	1967
Prince	1968-70
Streamliner 2nd & 3rd versions	1968-75
Van Eps seven-string 1st & 2nd versions	1968-78
Van Eps six-string	1968-72
Roc Jet 1st & 2nd versions	1969-79
Deluxe Chet	1972-73
Super Chet	1972-80
Roc II	1973-75
Country Roc	1974-79
White Falcon 4th version	1974-78
White Falcon Stereo 5th version	1974-78
Broadkaster semi-hollow body 1st & 2nd versions	1975-79
Broadkaster solidbody version	1975-77
Atkins Axe	1977-80
Committee	1977-81
Super Axe	1977-80
TK300	1977-81
Beast BST-1000	1979-81
Beast BST-2000	1979-80
Beast BST-5000	1979-81
Beast BST-1500	1981
Country Squire	1981
Country Club 1955 Custom 6196-1955	1995-99
Nashville 1955 Custom 6120-1955	1995-99
White Falcon 1955 Custom 6136-1955	1995-99
Nashville 1955 Custom Western 6120W-1955	1997-99
Spectra Sonic C Melody Baritone 6144	2002-current
Spectra Sonic Lead 6143	2002-current
Nashville Western 6120WCST	2004-current
White Falcon 6136CST	2004-current

JAPAN

Country Classic I 6122S	1989-2003
Country Classic II 6122	1989-current
Duo Jet 6128	1989-current
Jet Firebird	1989-current
Nashville 6120	1989-current
Nashville Western 6120W	1989-2003
Round Up 6121	1989-2003
Silver Jet 6129	1989-current
Tennessee Rose 6119	1989-current
White Falcon 6136	1989-current
White Falcon 7593	1989-current
White Falcon 7594	1989-current
Black Falcon 6136BK	1992-98, 2003-current
Black Falcon 7593BK	1992-98, 2003-current
Black Falcon 7594BK	1992-98
Nashville 6120-1960	1992-current
Rancher 6022CV	1992-99
Synchromatic 400MCV	1992-2001
Anniversary one-pickup	1993-98
Anniversary two-pickup	1993-current
Country Classic II 6122-1962	1993-current
Nashville Brian Setzer	1993-current
Tennessee Rose 6119-1962FT	1993-current
White Penguin	1993-94, 2003-current
Duo Jet 6128-1957	1994-current
Silver Jet 6129-1957	1994-current
Synchromatic 400CV	1994-2002
Synchromatic 6040MC-SS	1994-current
Axe	1995-2001
Silver Falcon 6136SL	1995-current
Silver Falcon 7594SL	1995-98
Sparkle Jet 6129T	1995-current
Country Classic 6122-12 12-string	1996-2001
Malcolm Young I 6131SMY	1996-current
Malcolm Young I 6131SMYF	1996-current
Malcolm Young I 6131SMYR	1996-current
Malcolm Young II 6131SMY	1996-current
Malcolm Young II 6131SMYF	1996-current
Malcolm Young II 6131SMYR	1996-current
Nashville Junior 6120JR	1996-98
Nashville Junior 6120JR2	1996-current

Silver Jet 6129T-1962	1996-current
Sparkle Jet 6129-1957	1996-2002
Country Classic 6122-1958	1997-current
Duane Eddy 6120DE	1997-2003
Duane Eddy 6120DEO	1997-2003
Nashville 6120-6/12 double neck	1997-current
Country Classic Junior 6122R	1998-current
Duo Jet 6128T-6/12 double neck	1998-current
Super Gretsch 7690	1998-2002
Nashville Brian Setzer Hot Rod 6120SH	1999-current
Nashville Keith Scott 6120KS	1999-current
Tennessee Rose 6119-1962HT	1999-current
White Falcon Junior 7594JR	1999-2002
Bo Diddley 6138	2000-current
Elliot Easton 6128TBEE	2000-current
Elliot Easton 6128TEE	2000-current
Elliot Easton 6128TREE	2000-current
White Falcon Stephen Stills 6136-1958	2000-current
Country Club 6196	2001-current
Duo Jet 6128T-1962	2001-current
Nashville western 6120W-1957	2001-current
Anniversary Junior 6118JR	2002-current
New Jet 6114	2002-03
New Nashville 6120N	2002-03
Anniversary 6118T-120	2003-current
Black Penguin 6134B	2003-current
Country Club 6192	2003-current
Country Club 6193	2003-current
Nashville Classic 6122-1959	2003-current
Nashville Double Cutaway 6120DC	2003-current
Nashville Dynasonic 6120DS	2003-current
Nashville Dynasonic Western 6120DSW	2003-current
Round Up 6121W	2003-current
Tennessee Special 6119SP	2003-current
Anniversary Junior 6118TJR	2004-current
Black Falcon 6136TBK	2004-current
Country Classic Special 6122SP	2004-current
Country Club 6193T	2004-current
Country Club 6196T	2004-current
Jet Firebird 6131T	2004-current
Nashville Golden Anniversary 6120GA	2004-current
White Falcon 6136T	2004-current

KOREA

Historic Series Streamliner	1999-2003
Historic Series Synchromatic	1999-2003
Historic Series Thinline Synchromatic	1999-2003
Electromatic Bo Diddley	2000-current
Electromatic Double Jet 1st version	2000-03
Electromatic Jet Club	2000-03
Electromatic Jet Pro	2000-03
Electromatic Jet Sparkle	2000-03
Electromatic Jet Sparkle F/Hole	2000-03
Electromatic Junior Jet 1st version	2000-03
Electromatic Junior Jet II 1st version	2000-03
Synchromatic Bo Diddley	2000-03
Synchromatic Double Jet	2000-03
Synchromatic Jet Club	2000-03
Synchromatic Jet Pro	2000-03

Synchromatic Jet II	2000-03
Synchromatic Junior Jet	2000-03
Synchromatic Sparkle Jet	2000-current
Synchromatic Sparkle Jet F/Hole	2000-current
Historic Series Synchromatic Jr	2001-03
Synchromatic Elliot Easton	2002-03
Synchromatic Jet Baritone	2002-03
Synchromatic Sparkle Jet Double Neck	2002-03
Electromatic Double Jet 2nd version	2004-current
Electromatic Elliot Easton	2004-current
Electromatic Jet Baritone	2004-current
Electromatic Jet Double Neck	2004-current
Electromatic Junior Jet 2nd version	2004-current
Electromatic Junior Jet II 2nd version	2004-current
Electromatic Hollow Body	2004-current
Electromatic Pro Jet	2004-current
Electromatic Special Jet	2004-current

INDEX

A page number between 108 and 133 indicates an entry in the Reference listing of all models.

An *italic* page number indicates an illustration.

A

AC/DC *74-75*, 93
acoustic guitars 9
Adams, Bryan 93
Adjustamatic bridge 134
American Orchestra acoustic 9
Anniversary *34*, 52, 97, 104, 108, 109, 113, 114, 122
Anniversary Stereo 109
Arm, Mark 91
Astro-Jet *58-59*, 64, 129
Ash, Sam *see* Sam Ash model
Atkins Axe 85, 97, 130
Atkins, Chet *18*, *19*, 25, 28, 29, *35*, 40, 41, 44, 48, 49, 65, 73, 76, *79*, 80, 85, 89, 93, 96-97,
Axe 97, 131

B

Bachman, Randy 104
Baldwin company 72-73, 76, 77, 84, 88, 89, 92
banjos 9, 32
baritone guitar 95, 101
baritone ukulele 25
Beast models *78*, 88, 89, 131
Beatles, The *43*, 65, 68
Beck, Jeff 15, 41
Bigsby vibrato 28, 41, 61, 77, 101, 134
Bikini 61, 128
Black Falcon 113, 126
Black Hawk 92, 123
Black Penguin 119
'Black Prince' 129
Blanda, George 104
Bo Diddley models 90, 96, 132
body styles 108
Bono *95*, 105
Booneviile factory 76, 88
bracing 49
Brian Setzer models: see Nashville Brian Setzer, Hot Rod
bridges 134
Britton, Chris *46*, 68
Broadkaster acoustic 9
Broadkaster drums 20

Broadkaster semi 84, 123
Broadkaster solidbody 84, 130
Brooklyn factory 9, 36-37, 69, 76
Buffalo Springfield 68
Burns 61, 77, 134, 136
Butts, Ray 44-45, 52, 84, 85
Byrds, The 68

C

Cadillac tailpiece 32
Caiola, Al *10*, 25
catalogues
   1950 *11*
   1955 *15*, *19*, *23*, 36
   1959 *35*
   1961 *39*, *51*, *55*
   1963 *47*, *55*
   1975 *74*
   1978 *79*
'Cat's Eye Custom' 109
Chet Atkins models: *see* Atkins Axe, Country Gentleman, Deluxe Chet, Nashville, 6120, Solid Body, Super Axe, Super Chet, Tennessean
China, manufacture in 97
chronology of models 140-141
Clapton, Eric *46*, 68
Clark, Roy 85
Clipper *30*, 108, 110
Cochran, Eddie *27*, 40, 96
Collingswood, Chris *99*, 105
Collins, Edwyn 92
colours 24, 32, 33
Committee *78-79*, 85, 89, 130
control layouts 21, 48, 53, 136
Convertible *31*, 36, 110
Corvette hollowbody *10*, 24, 108
Corvette solidbody *54*, *59*, 61, 77, 128, 129
Country Classic models *82-83*, 93, 105, 114, 126, 131
Country Club models *11*, 24, 33, 53, 57, 97, 104, 110, 111, 114
Country Club Stereo *39*, 53, 56, 97, 111
Country Gentleman *34-35*, *42-43*, *43*, 48, 49, 65, 89, 93, 96-97, 109, 123
Country Roc 81, 118
Crosby, David 68
Crosby Stills Nash & Young 84
Cult, The 92
Cure, The 92
custom colours 24, 33
custom shop 97, 104
cutaway(s) 16, 57, 61, 136

D

Danelectro 92
dating instruments 134-136
DeArmond, Harry 16, 17,
DeArmond pickups 16, 40, 41, 44, 45
Deluxe Chet 80, 81, 129
Depeche Mode 92
'dial up' mute 57
Diddley, Bo *26*, 41, 44, 77, 96 *see also* Bo Diddley models
Dorado brandname 84
double-neck 91, 97
drums 9, 13, 24, 69, 88, 92
Duane Eddy model 91, 96, 114
Duffy, Billy *83*, 92
Duffy, Dan 36, 76
Duncan, Seymour 100
Duo Jet *14*, *14-15*, 20-21, 25, *26*, *26-27*, 41, *50-51*, 65, 105, 118, 119, 127, 132
Dyna Gakki factory 105
DynaSonic pickup 16, 29, 100, 104

E

Easton, Elliot 96 *see also* Elliot Easton models
Eddy, Duane *27*, 40-41, *91*, 96 *see also* Duane Eddy model
Edwards, Clyde 80, 85
Electro II *10*, 16, 24, 108, 111
Electromatic (early model) 16, 24, 111
Electromatic brand (recent models) 97, *99*, 117, 120, 121, 128, 132, 133
Electromatic Spanish (early model) 12, 13, 16, 24, 108
Elliot Easton models 96, 119

F

factories
   Booneville, Arkansas 76, 88
   Broadway, Brooklyn, NYC 9, 36-37, 69, 76
   Dyna Gakki, Japan 105
   Middleton Street, Brooklyn, NYC 8, 9
   Ridgeland, SC 97
   South 4th Street, Brooklyn, NYC 8
   Terada, Japan 92
   Tokiwa, Japan 100, 101
fake f-holes 49, 77, 136
feedback 48
Fender 20, 24, 33, 72, 84, 97, 101, 104

Filter'Tron pickup 45, 48, 52, 84, 100
fingerboard markers 135-136
   half moon 32, 135
   hump-top 32
   Neo-Classic 52, 135
   thumbnail 52
'flip up' mute 57, 65
Floating Sound Unit (bridge) 60, 134
Fogerty, John 101
Fountains Of Wayne *99*, 105
Fred Gretsch Manufacturing Co 8
frets, number of 134
Frusciante, John 105

G

Gallup, Cliff *15*, 41
Garland, Hank *14*, 25
G-brand 21
George Harrison Model 68
Gibbons, Billy *103*
Gibson 16, 20, 24, 25, 33, 48, 53, 57, 61, 80, 84, 89, 93, 96
'Gold Duke' *59*, 77, 129
Goody, Sam *see* Sam Goody model
Gore, Martin 92
Grant, Phil 13, 76
Gretsch, Bill 12, 13
Gretsch, Fred Jr 12, 20, 73, 76, 89
Gretsch, Fred Sr 8-9, 12
Gretsch, Fred III 89, 92
Gretsch, Friedrich 8
Gretsch, Louis 9
Gretsch, Rosa 8
Gretsch, Walter 9
Gretsch & Brenner 9
Guitar Center dealer 97
Guitarama 17

H

Hagner, Bill 73, 76, 88
Hagner Musical instrument Corp 88
half moon markers 32
Harmony brand 24
Harrison, Dick 72
Harrison, George 26, *43*, 65, 68, 101, 105 *see also* George Harrison model
Harvey, P.J. *87*
Heat, Revd Horton 96
Hi-Roller 85
HiLo'Tron pickup 45, 101
Historic brand models 97, 108, 117
Hollow Body model *see* 6120
Hot Rod model 93, *94-95*, 100-101, 115

ACKNOWLEDGEMENTS

OWNERS' CREDITS

Guitars photographed came from the collections of the following individuals and organisations, and we are most grateful for their help. The owners are listed here in the alphabetical order of the code used to identify their instruments in the Key below. **AB** Andy Babiuk; **AH** Adrian Hornbrook; **AR** Alan Rogan; **AV** Arthur Vitale; **CA** Chet Atkins; **CC** Chinery Collection; **DC** Don Clayton; **DE** Duane Eddy; **DG** David Gilmour; **GD** Gary Dick; **GG** Gretsch Guitars; **GH** George Harrison; **GR** Gruhn Guitars; **JB** Jeff Beck; **JL** Jay Levin; **JR** John Reynolds; **JS** John Sheridan; **LW** Lew Weston; **MB** Mandolin Brothers; **MG** Music Ground; **MW** Michael Wright; **PD** Paul Day; **PI** Peter Ilowite; **SA** Scott Arch; **SR** Sunrise Guitars.

KEY TO INSTRUMENT PHOTOGRAPHS

The following key identifies who owned which guitars when they were photographed. After the relevant page number(s) we list the model followed by the owner's initials in **bold type** (for which see Owners' Credits above).
10: Electro II **LW**, Corvette **MB**. 10-11: Streamliner **AV**. 11: both Clubs **CC**. 14: Silver Jet **SA**, Jet Fire Bird **AR**, Duo Jet **GG**. 14-15: Duo Jet **JB**. 18: 6120 **SA**. 18-19: **CA**. 19: 6120 **CA**, Solid Body **LW**. 22: Penguin **CC**. 22-23: Falcon **SA**. 26: '58 Duo Jet **GG**. 26-27: '57 Duo Jet **GH**. 27: 6120 **DE**. 30: 6120 **GG**, Clipper **JR**. 30-31: Streamliner **JR**. 31: Convertible **CC**. 34: Anniversary two-pickup **GG**, one-pickup **AH**. 34-35: Gent **GG**. 35: Tennessean **GG**. 38: Falcon Stereo **SA**. 38-39: Falcon **GG**. 39: Club **JR**. 42: Tennessean **AB**. 42-43: Gent **GD**. 43: Gent **GD**. 46-47 Falcon **JR**. 50: gold Jet **DG**. 50-51: silver Jet **SA**. 54: Corvette **DC**. 54-55: Twist **SR**. 55: Princess **JL**. 58-59: Astro-Jet **PD**. 59: both Corvettes **PI**. 62: 12-String **JS**. 62-63: Monkees **JS**. 63: Viking **MG**. 66-67: Van Eps **MG**. 67: Rally **GG**. 70: Roc **LW**. 70-71: Super **CA**. 74: Falcon Stereo **GG**, Falcon **MB**. 74-75: Roc **PD**. 78: Beast **MW**, Super **CA**. 78-79: TK 300 **PD**. 79: Committee **MW**. 82 onwards all **GG**.

Principal guitar photography is by Miki Slingsby and the pictures come from the Balafon Image Bank. The Astro-Jet, TK 300 and Country Roc were photographed by Garth Blore, and some pictures of recent guitars were supplied by Gretsch Guitars, photographed by Doug Crouch.

Memorabilia illustrated in this book – including advertisements, catalogues and record sleeves – is drawn from the Balafon Image Bank. Original items came from the collections of Chet Atkins, Tony Bacon, Jennifer Cohen, Paul Day, Gretsch Guitars, Gruhn Guitars, The Music Trades, National Jazz Archive (Loughton), and Alan Rogan.

Artist pictures were supplied by Redfern's, London, with the following exceptions: 27 (top) Duane Eddy; 38 (top left) Jennifer Cohen; 67 (top left) Tony Bacon; 82 (top) Ian Tilton; 103 Billy Gibbons.

Thanks (in addition to those named in Owners' Credits and Original Interviews): Julie Bowie; Walter Carter (Gibson); Dave Gregory; Jim Hilmar; Stan Jay (Mandolin Bros); Brian Majeski (The Music Trades); Stuart Maskell; Mike Newton; Julian Ridgway (Redfern's); Andrew Sandoval; Ian Tilton; Michael Wright.

Special thanks to Paul Day for his contributions to the vintage publication The Gretsch Book, upon which this work is based, and for the expertly revised reference section in this book. You're a prince, Paul. And to Mike Lewis at Gretsch Guitars – for all kinds of help.

Original interviews for this book were conducted by Tony Bacon as follows: Chet Atkins (April 1995, May 1995); Ray Butts (April 1995); Jennifer Cohen (April 1995); Dan Duffy (September 1995); Duane Eddy (April 1995); Ross Finley (April 1995); Phil Grant (August 1995); Fred Gretsch III (June 1995, July 2004); Bill Hagner (July 1995); Dick Harrison (July 1995, September 1995); Dale Hyatt (February 1992); TV Jones (July 2004); Duke Kramer (March 1995); Mike Lewis (July 2004); Ted McCarty (October 1992); Don Randall (February 1992); Dean Turner (March 1995), Paul Yandell (July 2004).

Books

Andy Babiuk Beatles Gear (Backbeat 2002)
Tony Bacon 50 Years Of Fender (Backbeat 2000), 50 Years Of The Gibson Les Paul (Backbeat 2002), The History Of The American Guitar (Friedman Fairfax 2001)
Tony Bacon (ed) Electric Guitars: The Illustrated Encyclopedia (Thunder Bay 2000)
Tony Bacon & Paul Day The Gretsch Book (Balafon 1996)
A R Duchossoir Guitar Identification (Hal Leonard 1990)
George Gruhn & Walter Carter Gruhn's Guide To Vintage Guitars (Miller Freeman 1999)
Dave Hunter (ed) Acoustic Guitars: The Illustrated Encyclopedia (Thunder Bay 2003)
Geoff Nicholls The Drum Book (Balafon 1997)
Jay Scott Gretsch: The Guitars Of The Fred Gretsch Company (Centerstream 1992)
Tom Wheeler American Guitars (HarperPerennial 1990)

Magazines Beat Instrumental (UK); Beat Monthly (UK); Cigar Aficionado (US); Country & Western Jamboree (US); Down Beat (US); Guitar Magazine (UK); Guitar Player (US); Guitarist (UK); Making Music (UK); The Music Trades (US); NME (UK); One Two Testing (UK); Vintage Gallery (US); Vintage Guitar Magazine (US); 20th Century Guitar (US).

Trademarks Throughout this book a number of registered trademark names are used. Rather than put a trademark or registered symbol next to every occurrence of a trademarked name, we state here that we are using the names only in an editorial fashion and that we do not intend to infringe any trademarks.

Updates? The author and publisher welcome any new information for future editions. Write to: Gretsch 50, Backbeat, 2A Union Court, 20-22 Union Road, London SW4 6JP, England, or email us: gretsch@backbeatuk.com

"Neil Young and I are going to go to Gretsch next couple of weeks. I think they were really amazed at the pure White Falcons we had, 'cos they're kind of old, both of them. So they offered to let us design one for them. And you know what the design is? There is no new design: just build the old one, man."
Stephen Stills, 1970